Afghanistan
From Cold War to Gold War

Asim Yousafzai, Ph.D., PG.

Copyright © 2013 Ace Publishing

Washington DC.

ALL RIGHTS RESERVED. This book contains material protected under International and US Federal Copyright Laws and Treaties. Any unauthorized reprint or use of this material is prohibited. No part of this book may be reproduced or transmitted in any form or by any means, electronic or mechanical, including photocopying, recording, or by any information storage and retrieval system without express written permission from the author / publisher.

The author can be contacted/followed **@asimusafzai** on Twitter or **Asim Yousafzai** on Facebook

ISBN-13: 978-0615923093

ISBN-10: 0615923097

DEDICATION

This book is dedicated to the memory of my mother who was there for us when nobody was around!

Contents

Preface	viii
Timeline of Major Events	xi
Acronyms	xviii
Miscellaneous Notes	xx
List of Figures	xxi
List of Photos	xxiii

Part-I
Regional and Historical Background

Chapter 1	The Afghan Elements	1
	The Inception of Afghanistan	1
	Pakistan and Afghanistan	8
	The Durand Line – A Virtual Border	10
Chapter 2	Modern Afghanistan	18
	Pre-Cold War (1919-1950)	18
	In the Heat of the Cold War (1950-1973)	20
Chapter 3	Afghanistan in Turmoil	22
	The Bloody Coups (1973-1979)	22
	The Soviet Occupation (1979-1989)	26
Chapter 4	Post-Soviet Afghanistan	30
	The *Mujahideen* Tug of War (1990-1996)	30
	Rise and Fall of Taliban (1996-2001)	31
Chapter 5	Afghan Society	35
	Ethno-linguistic Groups	35
	Pashtunwali	38

Chapter 6	Regional Players	42
	Pakistan	43
	Iran	45
	India	46
	Central Asian Republics	47
	China	47
	Russia	48

Part-II
Mineral and Water Resources

Chapter 7	Geology and Politics	52
	Afghan Geo-Politics	52
	Geology of Afghanistan	53
Chapter 8	Mineral Resources	60
	Rare Earth Minerals	61
	Heavy Metals	64
	Industrial Minerals	66
	Energy Resources	66
	Gemstones	68
	Challenges	69
Chapter 9	Water Resources	72
	Surface Water	73
	Kajaki Dam	76
	Salma Dam	80
	Ground Water	81
Chapter 10	Population and Resource Wars	90

Part-III
Present and Future

Chapter 11	The Insurgency	97
	Greater American Involvement	97
	Who Are Taliban?	100
	Can Taliban Be Defeated?	105
	Afghan War Asymmetry	108
	The "Pakistan" Problem	110
	The Poppy Culture	114
Chapter 12	The Afghan Government	124
	Afghan National Security Forces	125
	Afghan Corruption	133
	GIRoA and Reintegration	137
Chapter 13	Development	141
	Asymmetric Development	141
	Women Development	146
	Reconstruction and Development	154
	PRTs Role in Development	167
Chapter 14	US/NATO Departure on the Horizon	170
Chapter 15	Missed Opportunities	180
Chapter 16	The Way Forward	185
	American Legacy In Afghanistan	185
	Regional Solution	191
	The Elusive Future	195

Appendix A: Beginnings — 199

Appendix B: The Influence of Religion — 200

Appendix C: The reality of a Pakistani Nation — 203

Appendix D: An Introduction to Now Zad District, Helmand Province. Capt Michael C. Petit (USMC) — 205

Appendix E: Random Thoughts by a Civil Affairs Team Leader. Capt Michael C. Petit (USMC) — 209

Appendix F: Recommendations for Civil Affair Teams. Capt Michael C. Petit (USMC) — 212

Appendix G: NATO Bases as Wealth Spreading Machines. Metin Tarcan (2009) — 217

References — 219

Index — 229

Preface

I wrote this book after an endless search for some written material which can point me in the right direction as to how we arrived at the present fiasco in Afghanistan. I exhausted all my options on online and offline resources with no luck. I decided to write this book to fill in that void. This book provides an overview of the Afghan issue and explains why it has become a 'Graveyard of Empires'. The book explains Afghanistan's transition from a Cold War era to one where mineral wealth could be the next target for Super Powers. The book should be used as a general reference only as nothing has been described in detail. It is intended for general readers; even the scientific topics are written with the interest of a general reader in mind. The unique feature of the book is that history and international politics have been combined with natural resources for the first time under one title. Original pictures from the scene aid in understanding the conundrum.

Most of the material in this book came directly from my interaction with ordinary Afghans, government officials and most importantly US and NATO military personnel working in Afghanistan. I have placed more emphasis on the southern part of the country where the Taliban insurgency is strong. Over the course of my research for this book, I was starkly reminded of the fact that most military and civilian personnel have no idea why the Afghans behave the way they do. Ironically, most military officials also have no clue why they are there in the first place! Regardless of their knowledge of the Afghan quagmire, I salute their dedication to the invaluable service they have been providing since the war began in late 2001.

The book is divided into three parts detailing the history of the Afghan war; the present scenario and whether we can predict a future by looking at its bloody history. What kind of lessons the

US/NATO officials learned from the Afghan adventure have been detailed throughout the book. As a native Pashtun, I grew up in Peshawar and witnessed the rise and fall of military dictatorships, religious extremism and the plight of ordinary Pashtuns across the Durand Line. The first part of the book describes some of those experiences which are a direct result of my 20 years of working experience in the Afghanistan-Pakistan region. The second part of the book summarizes the untapped mineral wealth of Afghanistan and the efforts to control its natural resources. Situation on the ground is discussed in some detail in the third part of the book along with a roadmap towards the uncertain future.

The book can prove to be a great resource for anyone currently working in Afghanistan or who intends to work there in the near future. Military personnel can especially benefit from the contents as they are concise and summarize the major events in the past and present. It can also prove to be a good starting point for geoscience professionals and those who are working on the natural resources in general.

I am indebted to Michael C. Petit (Capt, USMC) for sitting with me for innumerable hours of fruitful discussions about the Afghan war. We blew hundreds of cigars while sitting in a wooden cabin rattled by the boom of exploding IEDs on a military base in northern Helmand. His Civil Affairs team was a source of inspiration for the local Afghans. I would like to thank Gunnery Sargent Timothy A. Noller (USMC) for keeping me on track for finishing this book. Thanks are due to Stacey Altamirano for editing the language of the first part of the book. Thanks to Qasim Yousafzai who edited the journalistic aspects of the manuscript and offered invaluable suggestions for improvement. I thank all the military and civilian personnel who spoke to me on and off the record.

Dr. Asim Yousafzai
Washington, DC.

Timeline of Major Events

1526	Zahiruddin Muhammad Babar conquers India through Khyber Pass and establishes the Mughal Rule
1601	British East India Company (EIC) arrives in the Indian subcontinent
1612	Mughal Emperor Nurruddin Salim Jehangir signs a treaty with the EIC giving them exclusive rights to start building factories in Bengal (Now Bangladesh and eastern India)
1747	Ahmad Shah Abdali (Durrani) establishes his dynasty in Afghanistan
1757	Bengal ruler Nawab Siraj Ud Daulah is defeated by the British forces in the Battle of Plassey
1839-1842	The First Anglo-Afghan war causes the English their first comprehensive defeat on the Indian soil and thus the "Great Game" begins
1857	The Indian communities jointly organize a rebellion (known as the Indian Mutiny) against the EIC rule with an aim to take back India from the foreign elements.
1858	The EIC rule ends and the British Crown declares the Indian subcontinent as its new colony
1878-1880	The English secures partial control of Afghanistan and the Afghan government agrees to cede their foreign policy to the British.
1893	The Durand Line is demarcated as the *de facto* boundary between Afghanistan and British India
1919	The Third Anglo-Afghan war results in victories for both Afghans and the English and eventually leads to the end of the "Great Game"
1919	Lenin calls Amanullah Khan the 'Leader of Only Independent Islamic State' and encourages him to

	rally enslaved Muslims around the world for independence
1921	The Afghans declare complete independence from the British and modern Afghanistan comes into being with Amanullah Khan as its first King
1921	the Afghan-Soviet Treaty of Friendship is signed
1924	The Soviets provides King Amanullah with fighter planes to eliminate antagonism to the king's modernization
1929	Tajik leader Habibullah Kalakani (*Bachae Saqaw*) declares himself the King after a revolt which ousted Amanullah Khan
1929	*Bachae Saqaw* is hanged on November 1, 1929 and Nader Shah is proclaimed the new King of Afghanistan
1933	Nader Shah assassinated and his son Muhammad Zahir Shah is made the new King who rules until 1973
1947	Pakistan and India declare independence from the British Rule
1948	M. A. Jinnah, the creator of Pakistan, dies
1948	Kashmir becomes disputed and India and Pakistan go to war. Line of Control (LoC) is established
1953	King Zahir Shah appoints his first cousin Prince Daud as the prime minister
1964	"New Democracy Program" is introduced which includes formation of a constitution, a bi-cameral parliament, free elections, free press and freedom to form political parties
1965	Second Indo-Pak war, Afghanistan remains neutral
1971	East Pakistan declares independence from West Pakistan and is called Bangladesh after hundreds of thousands of Pak Army soldiers accept defeat and surrender to the Indian Army in the capital Dhaka

1973	Daud organizes a coup while the King is in Italy for medical reasons. Daud makes a public broadcast declaring Afghanistan a republic and himself as the first President of the Republic of Afghanistan in July
1977	The elected prime minister of Pakistan, Zulfiqar Ali Bhutto, is jailed by the ultra-conservative Army General Zia ul Haq and later hanged by the military who stages a coup in July
1978	Daud and his entire royal family, including children and grandchildren, are murdered on April 28, thus bringing an end to the Mohammadzai tribe rule in Afghanistan
1979	Shah Reza Pehlavi of Iran is toppled by the Islamic Revolution of Ayatullah Khomeni in February
1979	In Pakistan, General Zia indicts Mr. Bhutto in a reportedly false homicide case and gets him hanged on April 04
1979	Hafeezullah Amin and Noor Muhammad Taraki, leaders of PDPA, are busy plotting against each other and trying to secure the Russian support
1979	In August, a large number of Russian military advisors enter Kabul to maintain peace. Amin is kills a sleeping President Taraki and declares himself as the President in October
1979	On December 27, a full-fledged Russian invasion takes place and Hafeezullah Amin is killed in the presidential palace
1979	Babrak Karmal declares himself as the new chief of PDPA and is installed as the president of Afghanistan. The country becomes officially known as the Democratic Republic of Afghanistan
1980	Cold War at its peak. The West, Gen Zia and ISI are busy organizing the *Mujahideen* against the Red Army and an all-out war engulfs Afghanistan

1984	Wealthy Arabs, including Osama Bin Laden (OBL), join the Mujahideen resistance against the Russians. Al-Qaeda is born
1986	Babrak Karmal is replaced by Dr. Najibullah who served as the chief of secret police
1987	The Russians realize that the war cannot be won and an exit strategy is worked out
1988	Geneva Accord is signed in May to put an end to the Afghan war
1988	August 17 saw the departure of General Zia from the scene when his military plane exploded midair killing him and 17 other top brass military personnel. And the US ambassador to Pakistan
1988	Benazir Bhutto, daughter of the Zulfiqar Bhutto is elected as the first woman Prime Minister in an Islamic country
1992	The communist government of Najibullah falls as *Mujahideen* advance towards Kabul
1994	The people of Kandahar and adjoining areas choose *Mullah* Omar as their spiritual and military leader (Supreme Commander) in and he assumes the title of Amirul Momineen (Commander of the faithful Muslims)
1996	Rise of a dark force called the Taliban (madrassa students) under *Mullah* Omar. Kabul falls to Taliban on September 27
1996	Najibullah is hanged in the main square and his body is dragged in the streets of Kabul by the victorious Taliban
1999	Army General Pervez Musharraf topples the elected government of Nawaz Sharif and imposes military rule in Pakistan
2001	March 21, Bamiyan *Buddhas* destroyed by Taliban
2001	Anti-Taliban leader Ahmad Shah Massoud is killed on September 9

2001	September 11, America comes under attack from al-Qaeda. Terrorism is spreading its tentacles outward from Afghanistan
2001	October 7, first US air strikes on Taliban targets
2001	Taliban defeated in December and an interim setup is installed
2003	*Loya Jirga* is convened in Kabul electing Hamid Karzai as the President of the transitional setup
2003	US invades Iraq on March 19 leaving Karzai government on his own
2004	Hamid Karzai elected as the President in general elections
2007	Tehreek-e-Taliban Pakistan (TTP) created
2007	USGS announces preliminary assessment of the Afghan mineral wealth
2008	Mumbai hotel came under attack from Lashkare Taiba (LeT), a terrorist organization based in Pakistan
2009	US Troop surge for Afghanistan announced
2009	December, An al-Qaeda double agent kills seven CIA operatives in a US base in Khost
2010	Wikileaks releases secret documents in July
2010	Lisbon summit in November sets 2014 as the troop withdrawal date from Afghanistan
2011	OBL killed in a Seal's operation in Abbottabad, Pakistan, on May 1
2011	Ex-President Rabbani assassinated in September
2011	Salala incident takes place in November in which NATO troops kill 24 Pak Army soldiers on the Afghan border
2012	Afghans in general and Taliban in particular were enraged by US Marines reportedly urinating on three insurgent corpses in January
2012	Major protests in the Af-Pak region in February over reported burning of Quran at a military base

2012	Green on Blue incidents continue with massacre at FOB Delhi in Garamser District in August
2013	Afghan forces take control of the country's security from NATO
2013	TTP chief Hakimullah Mehsud killed in a suspected US drone strike in October enraging the Pakistani public and establishment
2014	Afghanistan enters into yet another transitional phase, this time from Cold War to Gold War!

Acronyms

AGS: Afghan Geological Survey
ALP: Afghan Local Police
ANA: Afghan National Army
ANCOP: Afghan National Civil Order Police
ANP: Afghan National Police
ANSF: Afghan National Security Forces
AO: Area of Operation
ARRP: Afghan Reintegration and Reconciliation Program
ATT: Afghan Transit Trade
AUP: Afghan Uniformed Police
BSO: Battle Space Owner
BRAC: Bangladesh Rural Advancement Committee
CAG: Civil Affairs Group
Capt: Captain
CARs: Central Asian Republics
CERP: Commander's Emergency Response Program
CF: Coalition Forces
CIA: Central Intelligence Agency
CID: Criminal Investigation Department (Afghanistan)
CNPA: Counter Narcotics Police of Afghanistan
Col: Colonel
COIN: Counter Insurgency
CTP: Counter Terrorism Police (Afghanistan)
DACAAR: Danish Committee for Aid to Afghan Refugees
DAIL: Department of Agriculture, Irrigation and Livestock (Afghanistan)
DCOP: District Chief of Police (Afghanistan)
DG: District Governor (Afghanistan)

DoD: Department of Defense (United States)
DST: District Stabilization Team
EIC: East India Company
FATA: Federally Administered Tribal Areas
FET: Female Engagement Team
GIRoA: Government of the Islamic Republic of Afghanistan
GySgt: Gunnery Sargent (USMC)
HAVA: Helmand Arghandab Valley Authority (Afghanistan)
IED: Improvised Explosive Device
IGO: International Governmental Organization
IOTV: Improved Outer Tactical Vest
IRD: International Reconstruction & Development
ISAF: International Security and Assistance Force
ISI: Inter-Services Intelligence (Pakistan)
J&K: Jammu and Kashmir
KP: Khyber Pukhtunkhwa (formerly NW Frontier Province, Pakistan)
L.Cpl.: Lance Corporal
LoC: Line of Control (Pakistan)
Lt. Col: Lieutenant Colonel
MAAWS-A: Money As A Weapon System – Afghanistan
MEF: Marine Expeditionary Force
MoM: Ministry of Mines (Afghanistan)
MEW: Ministry of Energy and Environment (Afghanistan)
NATO: North Atlantic Treaty Organization
NGO: Non-governmental Organization
NWFP: Northwest Frontier Province (Pakistan)
OBL: Osama Bin Laden
PDPA: Peoples' Democratic Party of Afghanistan
PRT: Provincial Reconstruction Team

REEs: Rare Earth Elements
Sgt: Sargent
SRAD: Southern Regional Agricultural Development
TTP: Tehreek-e-Taliban Pakistan (Pakistan Taliban Movement)
UN: United Nations
USAF: United States Air Force
USAID: United States Agency for International Development
USD: US Dollar
USDA: United States Department of Agriculture
USGS: United States Geological Survey
USMC: United States Marine Corps
USSR: Union of Soviet Socialist Republics

Miscellaneous Notes

1. Units of distance: mile/feet (1 mile = 1.6 kilometer; 1 meter = 3.39 feet)

2. Foreign language words have been italicized.

3. Some of the names and designations have been switched to maintain confidentiality.

4. All photo have been taken by the author during 2011-12 except otherwise mentioned.

List Of Figures

Figure 1: Regional map showing Afghanistan's neighbors (From: Maps of World).   3

Figure 2: The extent of British-Indian Empire (From: Historical Atlas of the British Empire).   7

Figure 3: Durand Line marks an unstable border between Pakistan and Afghanistan (Modified from Google Maps).   11

Figure 4: Ethno-linguistic subdivisions in Afghanistan and surrounding countries (From: ISW, 2009).   38

Figure 5: Geologic Time Scale with ages given in millions of years.   56

Figure 6: Physiography of Afghanistan.   57

Figure 7: Afghan mineral development projects (From: Randall and Owen, 2012).   58

Figure 8: Simplified tectonic map of Afghanistan showing various terranes and the Logar Ophiolite Complex (From: Benham et al., 2009).   58

Figure 9: Tectonic elements in the Afghan Block.   59

Figure 10: Results of aerial geophysical survey conducted by US Naval Research Lab (From: Burgess, 2006).   64

Figure 11: Location map of Ainak copper deposit.   65

Figure 12: Amu Darya (River Amu) petroleum basin.   68

Figure 13: Major regional River Systems
(From: University of Texas).   76

Figure 14: Major cities in Afghanistan   145
(From: Afghan diaspora).

List Of Photos

Photo 1: Afghan youth listening to speeches at an Elders' Shura in Kurghay (December 2011). 12

Photo 2: An Afghan youth is listening to a speech by an ISAF commander. 12

Photo 3: An Afghan elder is raising a question. 13

Photo 4: Afghan elders are discussing their problems with ISAF and government officials. 13

Photo 5: US Marines stand guard by an old non-functioning Russian tank in northern Helmand Province in October 2011. The tank is a reminder of the Red Army's defeat in Afghanistan. 28

Photo 6: The ISAF requires any trash to be burnt on all of its bases. 71

Photo 7: Officials from C-9, USAID, ISAF and Afghan Government are discussing strategy in the Water Summit at Camp Leatherneck, Helmand (February 2012). 74

Photo 8: The author presenting findings of his work at the Water Summit at Camp Leatherneck. 75

Photo 9: Aerial view of Helmand River as it enters the Kajaki dam (June 2012). 78

Photo 10: The picturesque Kajaki reservoir as seen from an ISAF chopper (June 2012). 78

Photo 11: Hanging wires from an electric pole is a

stark reminder of the Taliban hatred for civic amenities (November 2011). 79

Photo 12: Solar technology making inroads in rural Afghanistan (May 2012). 79

Photo 13: Solar panels for sale in a local bazar in Musa Qala (May 2012). 80

Photo 14: Diesel pumps discharge enormous amount of water depleting the aquifer at an alarming rate (Dahana, November 2011). 85

Photo 15: An Afghan child is filling in his water gallons with a hand pump from a drilled well. 85

Photo 16: The author measuring ground water quality and other physical parameters. 86

Photo 17: Aerial view of linear holes representing *karez* systems in northern Helmand. The holes are about 100 feet apart. 86

Photo 18: ISAF and DST officials trying to convince the locals to allow the construction of a check dam in Dahana. 87

Photo 19: The author is showing benefits of a check dam to the locals through the use of a physical model. 87

Photo 20: The author is inspecting the location for a check dam. 88

Photo 21: Mud cracks indicating desiccation in the

stream bed close to the location of the proposed
check dam.   88

Photo 22: The author is conducting field work on a
dried stream bed in a tributary of the Helmand River.   89

Photo 23: Truckloads of wheat seed and fertilizer
waiting to be distributed among the farmers of
Kandahar Province.   89

Photo 24: Relatives are identifying Taliban dead
bodies dumped outside of an AUP station
(January 2012). Some of them have been buried
in the graveyard in the background.   102

Photo 25: Afghan teenagers are playing popular
game *"Durra"* in which they hit each other with lashes
(Musa Qala, April 2012).   105

Photo 26: War asymmetry: Graveyard of
Mine-Resistant Ambush Protected (MRAP)
armored vehicles destroyed by Taliban IEDs
(December 2011).   108

Photo 27: Alternating fields of poppy and wheat in
Kandahar (April 2012).   116

Photo 28: Alternating fields of poppy and wheat in
Helmand (March 2012).   116

Photo 29: Large swaths of poppy covering fields in
Helmand.   117

Photo 30: Hashish (Cannabis) is normally grown

inside walled compounds to evade authorities
(Musa Qala, 2012). 117

Photo 31: Good times: DG Murad Saadat in a good
mood with an ISAF official (October 2011). 119

Photo 32: The author with Abdul Qayum, Deputy
governor Now Zad District (February 2012). 120

Photo 33: A long line of tractors parked at the DG's
compound waiting to be deployed for poppy
eradication (January 2012). 121

Photo 34: ISAF officials contributing to the local
economy (January 2012). 128

Photo 35: An off –duty policeman is smoking
hashish with little children around right in front
of his police station (Now Zad, 2012). 128

Photo 36: An ANP cop has hanged his AK-47 by
the barbed (concertina) wire while guarding a
DG's compound in northern Helmand (March 2012). 130

Photo 37: Governor Gulab Mengal of Helmand
Province inaugurating a newly renovated high school
for boys (August 2011). 134

Photo 38: Afghan children are sitting on the floor in a
high school. 134

Photo 39: FET members distributing supplies to mark
the inauguration of a school repaired with US money. 135

Photo 40: Two FET members and a member of USAID

at the inauguration of the school in northern Helmand.   135

Photo 41: Afghan nomad (*kochi*) girls standing in their dilapidated abodes in Khan Nashin (Photo by R. Khattak, April 2011).   142

Photo 42: Afghan women clad in *burkas/chadaris* (Photo by R. Khattak, May 2011).   147

Photo 43: Located in Helmand, an Afghan doctor is sitting in her clinic with scant facilities. The blood pressure monitor is not in working condition since its arrival (November 2011).   149

Photo 44: A US Marine is showing the use of dental hygiene to Afghan kids in Helmand (November, 2011).   149

Photo 45: A little girl suffering from an undiagnosed blood disorder is lying on a bed in her hometown of Khan Nashin because of lack of healthcare facilities (Photo by R. Khattak, June 2011).   150

Photo 46: A little girl sitting in unhygienic conditions in her home of Khan Nashin (Photo by R. Khattak, July 2011).   150

Photo 47: Home medicine is applied to a serious skin disease in a young boy (Photo by R. Khattak, August 2011).   151

Photo 48: Afghan kids are happy with dental hygiene products they received from the US Marine. (Photo by R. Khattak).   151

Photo 49: Women Center in northern Helmand

(December 2011). 152

Photo 50: A view of the 5000 USD beauty parlor in Now Zad District Center (November 2011). 152

Photo 51: High school teachers organized a student sit-in at the entrance of FOB Now Zad (March 2012) to demand airlifting of their teachers. 157

Photo 52: "Now Zad Choppers" building in the middle of nowhere (under construction). 163

Photo 53: Completed "Now Zad Choppers" building in the middle of nowhere. 163

Photo 54: Bridge to Nowhere! Two large buildings are being constructed in the middle of nowhere in Helmand Province. 164

Photo 55: Stolen vehicle worth 16,000 USD as ambulance parked in the DG's compound. 164

Photo 56: A US Marine is posing with the ambulance being used as a rooster house. 165

Photo 57: A rooster is enjoying his comfortable abode. 165

Photo 58: Dr. Ibrahim posing with US Marines after receiving the final installment of funds for his "ambulance" project. 166

Photo 59: A New Dawn; NATO tanks on their way out from northern Helmand (March 2011). 173

Photo 60: Little girls running a grocery store in northern Helmand (February 2012). 175

Photo 61: Fun times; A US Marine is hands up to a little kid with a toy gun (October 2011). 176

Photo 62: Grand Bargain; A teenager is trying to exchange his cell phone for the shades. 176

Photo 63: Afghans love for Martial Arts continues even during a bloody war (Now Zad, 2012). 177

Photo 64: The author with a group of US Marines (October, 2011). 183

Photo 65: Mayor Juma Khan looking at his renovated Bazar (December, 2011). 183

Photo 66: A USAID official is having an informal chat with Afghan children in Now Zad (October 2011). 187

Photo 67: Green on Blue friendship: An AUP cop with his Marine buddy (November 2011). 190

PART I
REGIONAL AND HISTORICAL BACKGROUND

Chapter 1 The Afghan Elements
The Inception of Afghanistan
Pakistan and Afghanistan
The Durand Line – A Virtual Border

Chapter 2 Modern Afghanistan
Pre-Cold War (1919-1950)
In the Heat of the Cold War (1950-1973)

Chapter 3 Afghanistan in Turmoil
The Bloody Coups (1973-1979)
The Soviet Occupation (1979-1989)

Chapter 4 Post-Soviet Afghanistan
The *Mujahideen* Tug of War (1990-1996)
Rise and Fall of Taliban (1996-2001)

Chapter 5 Afghan Society
Ethno-linguistic Groups
Pashtunwali

Chapter 6 Regional Players
Pakistan
Iran
India
CARs
China
Russia

Chapter 1
THE AFGHAN ELEMENTS

THE INCEPTION OF AFGHANISTAN

To understand the Afghan conflict and where does it stand today, one has to first take into account the regional geography, as traditionally, Afghanistan has been heavily influenced by all its neighbors. Afghanistan has a land area of approximately 251,825 square miles, slightly less than the entire state of Texas. It is a landlocked country with Pakistan to the south and east, Iran to the west, Central Asian Republics (CARs) to the northwest and Russia and China to the northeast. Afghanistan and the three CARs (Uzbekistan, Tajikistan and Turkmenistan) are the only countries in the region which do not have access to a water body (Figure 1).

According to the CIA World Fact book, the current estimated population of Afghanistan is a little more than 30 million. This country has never seen a completed census; the last one was carried out in 1979, which remained incomplete because of the Soviet invasion (cia.gov). It is a country of rugged mountains—dominated by Hindu Kush, the westernmost extension of Karakoram and Himalayas—and arid plains which become deserts in the south-west. As a result, like Pakistan, Afghanistan endures extreme temperatures. Afghanistan, being a landlocked country, has direct implications for the continued conflict in the region.

Afghanistan shares a 1200 mile long border with Pakistan, the longest of any of its neighbors. The border between the two countries was demarcated in 1893 by Sir Mortimer Durand and hence is known as the Durand Line (DL). A *Loya Jirga* (Afghan Constitutional Assembly) in 1949 declared the DL null and void and since then it has remained a bone of contention between the two countries.

Afghanistan shares a 500-mile long border with Iran and it has mostly remained a stable boundary. The shortest border lies with China in the northeast (~60 miles) through its panhandle called the Wakhan Strip in Badakhshan Province (Figure 1).

Figure 1: Regional map showing Afghan Provinces and immediate neighbors (From: University of Texas).

As with most global geographic issues today, the Afghanistan conflict can be traced back to the British colonial era. The Afghan problem must be studied in this context, otherwise empires will keep crumbling and the 'Graveyard of Empires' will keep on adding more tombstones. It all started when the British East India Company (EIC) arrived at the Indian subcontinent in 1601. EIC traded mainly in cotton, spices, silk, tea, opium and salt peter (a source for gun powder). Until the arrival of EIC, the Indians were unaware of the use of salt peter as a source for gun powder. The company was owned by English aristocrats and wealthy merchants. The Indian subcontinent (India, Pakistan, Bangladesh, Thailand and parts of Afghanistan) was under the Mughal rule which was established in 1526 by Zahiruddin Muhammad Babar, an ethnic Mongol/Turk. Babar was the first warrior to conquer India from the north through the Khyber Pass located along the DL.

To expand its trade, the EIC started to exert political influence by entering into agreements with the local rulers. The EIC quickly defeated their European trade rivals such as the Dutch and Portuguese trading companies. In 1612, Mughal Emperor Nurruddin Salim Jehangir signed a treaty with the EIC which gave them exclusive rights to start building factories in Bengal (Now Bangladesh and eastern India). The EIC continued its expansion throughout India and got a firm hold on political maneuverability. The Mughal rulers allowed EIC to expand its trade but the local population was averse to their political influence. The EIC continued to establish its sphere of influence over the next 150 years and managed to defeat the Bengal ruler Nawab Siraj Ud Daulah in 1757 in the battle of Plassey (the eastern part of Bengal is now the independent state of Bangladesh).

The EIC effectively began its Indian rule after winning this battle and continued its expansion policies in all directions. The EIC rule ended in 1858 when the British Crown declared the Indian subcontinent as its new colony. This is an important marker in the history of the Indian subcontinent and hence Afghanistan as well. In 1857, the Indian communities jointly organized a rebellion (known as Indian Mutiny) against the Company rule with an aim to take back India from the foreign elements. The Company was supported by their loyal employees and private militias who were better organized and thus defeated the poorly organized local groups. The loss in this "Freedom War" resulted in complete takeover of India by the British Crown and the British India Act was promulgated where EIC ceased to exist as a company and all the powers were transferred to the Crown.

The British continued their expansion policies towards the north and northwestern parts of the country. They easily captured areas up to the Indus River in the Himalayan foothills. In 1839, they decided to push towards the independent Pashtun (variously designated as Pukhtoon, Pakhtun, Pushtoon, Pashtun, and Pathan) tribes living on the eastern border of Afghanistan (Figure 2). The independent tribes offered a stiff resistance to the British Army onslaught. This war, known as the first Anglo-Afghan war (1839-1842), caused the English their first comprehensive defeat on the Indian soil and thus the "Great Game" started. The British were apprehensive of the expansionist Russian policies towards Afghanistan. The British-led Indian Army initially succeeded in this adventure, but towards the end of 1841, the Afghan tribes inflicted heavy casualties on the British Indian Army, killing and wounding thousands.

The second Anglo-Afghan war was fought between 1878 and 1880. This war also resulted in heavy losses (about 10,000 dead and injured) to the British Indian Army, but eventually the English were able to secure partial control of Afghanistan and the Afghan government agreed to cede their foreign policy to the British.

The third Anglo-Afghan war of 1919 resulted in victories for both sides and eventually led to the end of the Great Game. The British secured the reaffirmation of the DL, which was drawn on map in 1893 by Sir Mortimer Durand who served as the British India Foreign Secretary. In 1921, the Afghans declared complete independence from the British and modern Afghanistan came into being with Amanullah Khan its first King.

Even a cursory look at the Pre-World War I history indicates that Afghanistan is no stranger to conflict and warfare. Treason, switching sides and allies and opportunistic attitudes has been the rule rather than the exception. The Afghan soil remained a battleground between two imperial powers – Russia and Great

Britain – a trend that continues till this day. The only difference is that now a multitude of actors and players are involved.

The Indian subcontinent remained an English colony until 1947 when power was handed over to two independent nations; India and Pakistan. The British took away any commodities of economic significance back to their land during the entire presence from 1601 to 1947. This demonstrates the method through which empires are sustained by the plundering of others' wealth and natural resources. The span of recorded human history has shown that all major struggles are purely resource wars and whoever controls resources are the dominant powers.

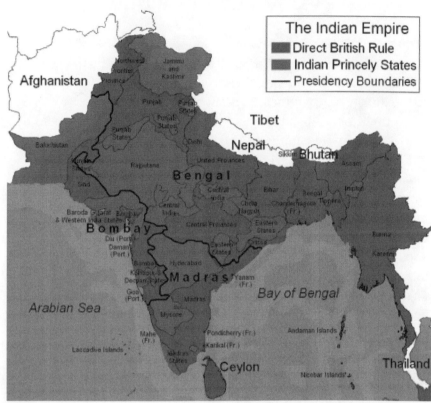

Figure 2: The extent of British-Indian Empire (From: Historical Atlas of the British Empire).

PAKISTAN AND AFGHANISTAN

Soon after World War II, a wave of independence swept the colonial territories. Eventually, after much struggle by the indigenous people, the British Crown decided to hand power back to the Indian communities. There were two dominant communities in British India and their coexistence was marked by a love-hate relationship. The Muslims had ruled India from 1526 - 1857 and they wanted to regain some of that glory back. The Indian soil was sliced into two (1947) or (three-1971) parts; one would be called Pakistan with majority of Muslims and the Hindu majority areas would be called India. Interestingly, there were two distinct Muslim majority areas – both became the eastern and western parts of Pakistan separated by a thousand miles of Indian territory. It is interesting to note that the eastern portion of Pakistan declared its independence from West Pakistan in 1971 and became the independent state of Bangladesh. This separation caused a severe blow to the very theory under which a separate Muslim majority homeland was established (The Two-Nation Theory).

In 1946, a boundary commission was set up by the British government to demarcate various boundaries. The decision on the border between India and West Pakistan was a particularly thorny one and has led to one of the two oldest territorial issues on the map; the other one being Israeli-Palestinian conflict. India and Pakistan did not agree on the fate of Jammu and Kashmir (J&K); a Muslim majority state but with a Hindu ruler (*Maharaja*). India laid claim to it while Pakistan declared Kashmir as its integral part as it was a Muslim majority state. In 1948, India and Pakistan fought their first war and the state of Kashmir was divided into two parts – one controlled by each country and the two halves separated by a Line of Control (LoC; not an international border). Besides other issues, this contested border has led to two more wars between the two countries and has direct implication for the Afghan conflict.

Strategically, the state of J&K is extremely important as this is the only region where India is separated from China. These two countries have had military and economic rivalries for the past several decades. The state of J&K remains a thorny issue between India and Pakistan and since both countries are nuclear-armed, it was called the "most dangerous country in the world" in 2007 by Newsweek Magazine in its cover story. Since then, things have turned for the worst; every inch of the country is a breeding ground for intolerance, extremism and terrorism including the capital Islamabad.

Since 1947, Pakistan has adopted a policy to bring down India in any possible way in order to force India to give up the contested region of J&K. Pakistan has used all possible means to destabilize the J&K region – from suicide bombings to direct military intervention to train members of *Jihadi* organizations in ISI (Inter-Services Intelligence) camps. Pakistan even managed terror attacks inside India; the Mumbai Hotel attacks of 2009 are a prime example. The rivalry between these two nuclear neighbors is primarily carried forward by bureaucracies and militaries; the general public has remained friendly to a large extent.

The British departed in 1947, leaving behind their political and economic systems. India adopted the British system according to its needs while Pakistan has tried to reconcile it with Islamic laws. Subsequently, other ethnic and religious groups got their priorities right and started their own rebuilding. Indian Hindus have always been introvert and very faithful to their motherland. To them, the Indian soil is everything. Indian Muslims faced the dilemma of choosing either local customs and traditions or follow Arabia. Except a few open minded liberals, every Muslim favored following the Arabs rather than contending themselves and remaining faithful to their own soil. This unnatural experimentation has created many issues and solved very few.

Indian Muslims have maintained a separate identity and that was the main reason why they overwhelmingly supported the idea of splitting their own soil into pieces after the British left in 1947. Once they got their own country in 1947, they continued with their Pan-Islamist dreams and creating a great *Khilafah* (Kingdom of Islam) once again. The accumulation of *Jihadi* terrorists in Pakistan and Afghanistan is a natural continuation of this effort.

THE DURAND LINE
A Virtual Border

The Indus River has been historically seen as the western boundary of India. The region up to the Oxus River was dominated by Pashtuns (Photos 1-4), who have always taken pride in a recorded history going well before 2000 B.C. (Mahmud, 2010). Traditionally, Pashtuns comprise a single racial group occupying a strategically vital region extending from Swat and Indus Valley through the Tribal belt into northern and southern Afghanistan. When the British extended their empire to the Khyber Pass, they did not face any stiff resistance. They did hit a brick wall when Pashtun tribes living in the region adjoining Afghanistan (Figure 3) started to resist the British Indian forces.

Afghanistan was founded by Ahmad Shah Abdali (Durrani) in 1747. However, the country has lacked its own identity since its creation as it was surrounded by Indians, Persians, Turks, Mongols and Chinese. Afghanistan, being comprised of mixed ethnicities, was called a "purely accidental state" by the British Viceroy, Lord

Curzon. The British decided to create a buffer zone, currently known as FATA (Federally Administered Tribal Areas), between the Indian empire and Afghanistan.

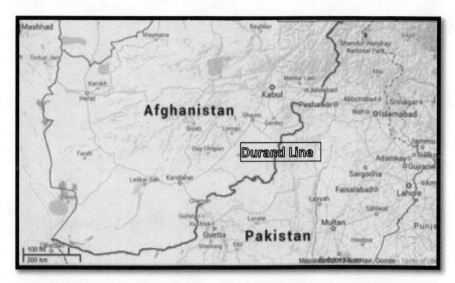

Figure 3: Durand Line marks an unstable border between Pakistan and Afghanistan (Modified from Google Maps).

Photo 1: Afghan youth listening to speeches at an Elders' Shura in Kurghay (December 2011).

Photo 2: An Afghan youth is listening to a speech by an ISAF commander.

Photo 3: An Afghan elder is raising a question.

Photo 4: Afghan elders are discussing their problems with ISAF and government officials.

In 1893, Sir Mortimer Durand (British India foreign Secretary) and *Amir* Abdul Rehman of Afghanistan signed a treaty marking the buffer zone and since then it has been known as the Durand Line (DL). This proved to be a good deal for the Afghan King as he received a number of concessions from the British government. It was also decided that whenever these tribes want, this zone would cease to exist. The zone was marked on paper and still exists on paper only. There is no physical barrier or fence along this 1200 mile long border (Figure 3). On the Indian side of the DL, the area was divided into a number of administrative divisions called Agencies roughly along intra-tribal divisions. When Pakistan came into being in 1947, its government continued to extend full autonomy to the FATA region. The autonomy to Pashtun tribes continues till this day and it remains a no-man's land.

The British decided to create a buffer zone here rather than a boundary line as the ethnicities were the same on either side. The British followed a policy of appeasement towards the Pashtun tribes on the Indian side of the border. They favored them heavily and appointed special quotas for them in various branches of the government including the military. Cullather (2002), described the effect of DL on the Pashtuns as follows; "By bisecting tribal homelands......the DL restricted Pashtun autonomy and facilitated new forms of indirect influence over peoples on both sides of it". This fact alone is a major problem for ISAF as the insurgents frequently cross the buffer zone and enter into Afghanistan from Pakistan.

In 1921, when Afghanistan declared independence from the British, the DL became the official border between British India and Afghanistan. However, since the Pashtun tribes lived across this border, it was never accepted as an international border, let alone an actual border. The tribes crossed the border at will. It is not always feasible to control international borders even with all the available technology – one case in point being the US-Mexico border. The DL was never recognized for political, cultural, social and economic reasons and therefore it only served as a "virtual border" and will continue to do so in the foreseeable future.

In 1947 when Pakistan declared independence and applied to the UN General Assembly for membership, the only negative vote was cast by Afghanistan. Afghanistan based its decision on the fact that Afghan tribes live across the DL and the areas up to the Indus River are a natural part of Afghanistan. It was demanded in the UN General Assembly that these border regions be settled before giving Pakistan a member status. Relations between Pakistan and Afghanistan, therefore, started on the wrong foot from day one. In 1949, a *Loya Jirga* (Grand Council) declared the DL Agreement as invalid. Pakistan, on the other hand, has always considered the DL as the international border between the two countries. "International Law states that boundary changes must be made among all concerned parties; and a unilateral declaration by one party has no effect. So, when in 1949, Afghanistan's "*Loya Jirga*" declared the DL Agreement invalid, it was considered a unilateral declaration, and therefore, could not be enforced. Furthermore, DL, like virtually any international boundaries, has no expiration date, nor is there any mention of such in the DL Agreement, which is contrary to the popular beliefs of certain Afghan scholars that the agreement lapsed in 1993 which is after a hundred years of its signing (Liveleak, 2012)".

Pakistan cannot afford to have two restive long borders; the other one being with India. Traditionally, Pakistan has always concentrated on its eastern border with India, its arch rival from the day they declared independence from the British. Afghanistan, being a landlocked country, is dependent on Pakistan for all trade needs. The easiest and cheapest way for Afghans to conduct trade is through ports in the Indian Ocean, the closest one being the Karachi port. Pakistan and Afghanistan signed an agreement known as Afghan Transit Trade (ATT) in 1967 to facilitate foreign trade. A thriving black market economy exists in the FATA due to tax evasion and smuggling facilitated by the ATT agreement. In 1999, the World Bank estimated the net value of this secret economy to be more than 30 billion USD a year. "This is one of the highest in the world and which successfully insulates local livelihoods from outside pressures" (Rashid, 2000). An entire auto industry is run on purely illegal basis in the FATA region. Pakistan has successfully used this agreement as leverage to control the Afghan government's desire to raise the DL issue.

Afghanistan has limited resources of its own and has always remained dependent on its neighbors for daily supplies. Its exports are limited to furs, dried and fresh fruits, rugs and wool while its poppy cultivation and drug export being an entirely separate issue. Limited resources have forced Afghanistan to be dependent on its immediate neighbors. This can be attributed to the tribal nature of Afghanistan. All Pashtuns are divided into major and minor tribes, and they are very protective of their tribal structure. As opposed to a nation-state, where there is a central authority, Afghanistan prides itself in a tribal structure where an individual's allegiance is first and foremost tied to his/her family and then to the tribe. Inter-tribal rivalries are a characteristic of this type of archaic societal structure.

Metin Tarcan (2009) considers state borders meaningless for tribes as tribesmen seasonally cross the borders with their flocks and smuggle goods of economic importance. Permeable borders provide sanctuary to the tribes by allowing them to cross to neighboring states. "The current problem in the Afghanistan–Pakistan border and the interactions between the members of the same tribe yet the citizens of different states explicitly reveal this dilemma" (Tarcan, 2009). Any effort at solving the DL issue can threaten the internal stability of either state as has been demonstrated on numerous occasions in the past. The tribes on either side of DL keep changing their allegiance; some support their governments, some support the Taliban and some are silent spectators. This is a manifestation of the survival mode in a tribal society.

Though the DL only exists on paper, yet its presence has created deep scars on the psyche of the Pashtuns in both Pakistan and Afghanistan. It is also a dilemma for those Pashtuns living in different countries around the world. Pashtuns on either side of the DL accuse each other of being brain washed. The Pashtu language has been influenced by Urdu and English on the Pakistani side and by Dari on the Afghani side of the DL. Some Pashtun groups, especially the ones on the eastern side of DL, believe that they are the real owners of Pashto and their language is the Standard Pashto. Rana Momand, a contemporary poet and writer, believes that our Pashto is influenced, but she believed in saving Pashtuns first and Pashto is eventually saved. "It's not our fault, our elders have done nothing to save our language, they never worked to give Pashto the status of official language; instead they were proud of speaking other languages".

Some analysts believe that they must first overcome pressing issues such as poverty, illiteracy, healthcare, gender disparity, war, discrimination, famine, infant mortality, life expectancy, hunger, fundamentalism, terrorism, just to name a few and only then tackle the linguistic issues.

Chapter 2
MODERN AFGHANISTAN

PRE-COLD WAR
1919 – 1950

Afghanistan declared independence from the British in 1921 after the third Anglo-Afghan war ended in 1919 with Amanullah Khan as its first king. Afghanistan remained relatively stable since its inception until 1973 when internal strife and civil wars took over. The country has seen periods of slow but steady development followed by periods of inactivity and relative discomfort. Since its independence, it has always maintained close diplomatic and economic ties with the then USSR. In 1919, soon after the war ended, Lenin called Amanullah Khan the 'Leader of Only Independent Islamic State' and encouraged him to rally enslaved Muslims around the world for independence. In 1921, the Afghan-

Soviet Treaty of Friendship was signed. In 1924, the Soviets provided King Amanullah with fighter planes to eliminate antagonism to the king's modernization. This is the first time, war planes were used on the Afghan soil. The first USSR invasion of Afghanistan took place in 1925 when Russia seized Utra Tangi Island located on Amu Darya (Amu River). After successful negotiations, the USSR returned the Island back to Afghanistan in 1926. This was followed by a treaty of neutrality and non-aggression with Afghanistan.

King Amanullah was an educated ruler and wanted to modernize his country, however, he was leading a group of people who were very conservative in their outlook. In early 1929, the people of Kabul rose against his regime and forced him out of Kabul. He moved back to his native town of Kandahar in his Rolls Royce. This was followed by a brief period of mayhem and a completely illiterate person by the name of Habibullah Kalakani declared himself the King. He is known in Afghan history as *Bachae Saqaw* – a literal translation for "an illiterate king". In mid-1929, General Nader Khan proceeded from Kandahar and regained Kabul from *Bachae Saqaw*. The illiterate king was hanged on November 1, 1929 and Nader Shah was proclaimed the new King of Afghanistan.

King Nader Shah was assassinated four years later and his son Muhammad Zahir Shah was made the new ruler of Afghanistan. His rule is the longest in Afghanistan's history and he is the only king who is still revered to this day in Afghanistan. He was educated in France, spoke French fluently, and came to the throne at the age of 19. The early years of his reign were dominated by the authority of his three uncles. The King recognized that Afghanistan faced two major problems: the need for more abundant food and for social evolution and amicable relations with all her neighbors (Wilber, 1953).

The Second World War did not change much for Afghanistan but the post war scenario brought new opportunities and challenges for a tribal society. King Zahir Shah witnessed the transformation of the south and central Asian region as it got divided into pro- and anti-Russian blocks.

IN THE HEAT OF THE COLD WAR
1950 – 1973

To broaden his support base, King Zahir Shah appointed his first cousin Prince Daud as the prime minister in 1953. Both men were liberal in their views and wanted a modern Afghanistan. To achieve their goals, Prince Daud sent his brother Prince Naim to the US to ask for military assistance. His appeal to Secretary of State John Foster Dulles did not bear fruit and the Afghan leaders turned to their neighbor USSR for help. The Soviets jumped on the opportunity as it aligned perfectly with their aspirations to get access to the "warm waters" of the Indian Ocean. Afghanistan fully leaned towards USSR in the period from 1955 to 1963.

Daud resigned as Prime Minister because King Zahir Shah was not willing to introduce reforms. The King eventually gave in and introduced "New Democracy Program" in 1964 which included formation of a constitution, a bi-cameral parliament, free elections, free press and freedom to form political parties. Soon thereafter, Noor Muhammad Taraki formed the People's Democratic Party of Afghanistan (PDPA). It was a party of Afghan urban elites with strong leanings to the communist ideology. Elections were held in 1965 for the first time in Afghanistan with only 10% of the population casting their votes. PDPA split into two factions in 1967; Taraki headed the Khalq party while Parcham was headed by Babrak Karmal. Afghans went to elections once again in 1969, this time the turnout being even lower. King Zahir

Shah held on to power and surrounded himself with loyalists while Prince Daud was busy organizing a coup which succeeded in 1973 while the King was in Italy for medical reasons. Daud made a public broadcast declaring Afghanistan a republic and himself as the first President of the Republic of Afghanistan in July 1973. The change in leadership did not bring any good omen for the Afghans as they remained focused on their internal chaos. The international scenario was now fully aligned along the lines of Pro-America or Pro-USSR camps and they were ready to fight their proxies. Afghanistan was once again in the cross hairs.

Chapter 3
Afghanistan In Turmoil

THE BLOODY COUPS
1973-1979

Afghanistan did not witness many peaceful days between 1973 and 1979 as there were conspiracies to hold on to power, bloody coups, military revolts and political slayings. President Daud proved to be the most destabilizing factor during this time period and at the end he and his country paid a hefty price. As with any head of state, Daud started to amass power after assuming the office of the president in 1973. He systematically rooted out leftist opposition and sent out many of them as ambassadors. In the next four years, he tried to forge a regional alliance in his favor and visited many countries including the USSR. However, he ended up losing the support of USSR as a result of his policies. In 1977 the two factions of PDPA were united with the help of USSR and decided to remove Prince Daud from power. The murder of Mir Akbar Khyber, a communist leader, proved a trigger in organizing mass protests in Kabul against the Daud regime. President Daud ordered the arrest of all protest leaders but was losing grip on power and eventually his own military turned against him. Daud and his entire royal family, including children and grandchildren, were murdered on April 28, 1978, thus bringing an end to the Mohammadzai tribe rule in Afghanistan.

The communist government took control in Kabul in May 1978 and was immediately rejected by the conservative population. The government announced land and social reforms which were rejected by the general public. The religious groups started to resist this new regime with arms. Events of early 1979 in neighboring Iran had a tremendous impact on Afghanistan. Shah Reza Pehlavi of Iran was toppled by the Islamic Revolution of Ayatullah Khomeni in February 1979, and the hostage situation that followed captured the American imagination while the events in Afghanistan were largely overlooked. Meanwhile, the Russians were closely watching the situation in both Iran and Afghanistan and were busy in heavy military buildup on the Afghan border. While the general public was busy fighting the communist regime throughout Afghanistan, the usual power struggle continued in the Kabul presidential palace.

Hafeezullah Amin and Noor Muhammad Taraki were busy plotting against each other and trying to secure the Russian support. In August 1979, a large number of Russian military advisors entered Kabul to maintain peace. Amin killed a sleeping President Taraki and declared himself as the President in October 1979. He immediately sought the support of USA against the Russian buildup. On December 24, 1979, a full-fledged Russian invasion took place and Hafeezullah Amin was killed in the presidential palace. Babrak Karmal declared himself as the new chief of PDPA and was installed as the president of Afghanistan. The country became officially known as the Democratic Republic of Afghanistan. The Red Army started a country-wide campaign to eliminate armed opposition to the new communist government. The religious groups which called themselves "freedom fighters" were at the forefront of this opposition and eventually became known as *"Mujahideen"* which translates as "people fighting for Allah". The Afghan Army had reached 100,000 strong before the war but had now dropped to 30,000 due to defection to *Mujahideen* (sounds familiar in the present scenario as well). Russia's long lived desire of getting access to the "warm waters" of the Indian Ocean was coming to fruition. Russian tanks rolled in to all parts of Afghanistan and the fighter jets soared into the Afghan airspace. Indiscriminate aerial and ground assaults led the Afghan population to flee to neighboring Pakistan and Iran. This is cited as the largest mass migration in recent history as 7 million Afghans became refugees.

The United Nations High Commission for Refugees (UNHCR) and other humanitarian assistance groups started a massive effort in providing shelter and food for these refugees. The city of Peshawar could not accommodate the influx of millions of refugees and therefore they spread to all corners of the country including the capital Islamabad and the mega-city of Karachi. The Afghans started to mingle into the Pakistani society and till this day hundreds of thousands of them are living in various parts of Pakistan. The Afghan refugees exerted a huge stress on the Pakistani infrastructure which was not sufficient for its own population to begin with. As of now almost two generations of Afghanis have grown up across the DL in Pakistan. The Afghan refugees were not only Pashtuns but Tajiks, Uzbeks, Turkmen and Hazara as well, they brought with them their own values and traditions which sometimes directly clashed with the local customs and traditions.

Some analysts believe that these refugees triggered the Talibanization of Pakistan. Living in refugee camps was not an easy experience for these Afghans, however, they received plenty of religious education there. The Afghan war created innumerable orphans and some of the refugee children were separated from their parents as well. These children attended madrassas in the refugee camps and later became a major part of the notorious terrorist group known as the Taliban.

Meanwhile, Pakistan also went through dramatic events and an elected prime minister was jailed and later hanged by the military who staged a coup in July 1977. The elected government of Zulfiqar Ali Bhutto was toppled by ultra-conservative Army General Zia ul Haq. General Zia indicted Mr. Bhutto in a reportedly false homicide case and got him hanged on April 04, 1979. All political activities were banned and Martial Law was imposed in the country. He later imposed a strict Sharia Law and banned music, alcohol and public display of affection or love. He started the process of Islamization of Pakistani society and religious leaders and *Mullahs* were given the highest positions in the government. Religious schools (Madrassas) were encouraged to be opened in every corner of the country. Zia's military regime also closely watched the events in neighboring Afghanistan. Zia was anxious to become a part of this conflict as his military regime was looking for legitimacy and international recognition. General Zia was about to become a central and most intriguing figure in the Afghan war. The entire south Asian region was passing through a period of turmoil.

THE SOVIET OCCUPATION
1979-1989

The stage was once again set for world powers to fight it out on the Afghan soil; only this time the Americans were at the forefront. As 1979 marks the first year of instability in the entire south Asian region, Afghanistan was especially hard hit. The Kabul Government started an active campaign of Sovietizing Afghanistan, while the *Mujahideen* were busy resisting such efforts. *Mujahideen* leaders moved their offices to Peshawar, just across the DL in Pakistan (see Figure 3). The military regime of General Zia and Pakistani spy agency The Directorate of Inter-Services Intelligence (ISI) got fully involved in patronizing the *Mujahideen* leaders which were divided into seven major groups. Professor Burhanuddin Rabbani, Sibghatullah Mojaddadi, Gulbuddin Hekmatyar, Abdul Rab Rasool Sayaf, Molvi Younas Khalis and Pir Syed Ahmad Gilani were the main figures leading the *Mujahideen* resistance groups operating out of Pakistan. Some of them were educated in Al-Azhar University of Cairo and had dreams of Pan-Islamism.

The United States and CIA came to the rescue of General Zia and ISI was given a free hand to run the affairs of the Afghan war. This is the beginning of a long collaboration between the two intelligence agencies. The Cold War had reached a new height as a result of the Afghan conflict. The CIA started supporting the *Mujahideen* resistance groups by funneling money and weapons through ISI. The refugee camps in Peshawar and elsewhere in Pakistan became recruiting grounds for the *Mujahideen* groups. The proxy war between USSR and United States has already begun on the Afghan soil. In May 1982, the US tried to consolidate the resistance groups under King Zahir Shah, but the effort failed on account of lack of ISI support. Afghans have traditionally never been united under one banner, and this effort was no exception. It was a perfect opportunity for ISI and Pakistani establishment to install a "friendly" government in Kabul to achieve that "strategic depth" which they have been dreaming about since their independence in 1947.

The Red Army began to spread to all corners of the country and the battle became fierce with mounting casualties on either side. The remnants of the Russian invasion can still be seen in various parts of Afghanistan (Photo 5). The Russians established security bubbles, concentrated on population centers (Population–centric COIN) and gave away money to the local Afghan commanders. It seems as if whatever the Americans have been trying for the past 12 years has already been done by the Russians with disastrous results for the Red Army and USSR.

Until 1984, only two regional powers were involved in the Afghan conflict; Iran and Pakistan. With the passage of time, the nature of the conflict was slowly changing to be perceived as a *Jihad* (holy war) against the infidels (Russians). Wealthy Arabs got involved in the conflict with their money and manpower. A wealthy Arab by the name of Osama Bin Laden (OBL) moved to Afghanistan along with his close friends and started fighting against the Russians. CIA and ISI fully supported Bin Laden and facilitated his movement across Afghanistan. Chechen and other Central Asian Jihadists joined the movement and Afghanistan became a breeding ground for men fighting a holy war. Meanwhile, Saudi Arabia and UAE (United Arab Emirates) stepped in to offset the Iranian influence, further exacerbating the Sunni-Shia dimension of the war.

Photo 5: US Marines stand guard by an old non-functioning Russian tank in northern Helmand Province in October 2011. The tank is a reminder of the Red Army's defeat in Afghanistan.

The combined weight of the anti-Russian forces was enough to turn the tide against the Red Army and the *Mujahideen* started to make significant gains in the war. The introduction of stinger missiles in the war proved to be a decisive factor in favor of *Mujahideen*. Babrak Karmal was replaced by Dr. Najibullah in 1986 who served as the chief of secret police. By 1987, the Russians realized that the war could not be won and started working on an exit strategy after fighting the war for seven years (unlike the Americans who are still fully involved in the war after 12 long years). Russian leaders were convinced that resolving Cold War issues with the west and initiating internal reforms were much more important that saving the communist government in Kabul.

The core principles for the Geneva Accord were signed in May 1988, which asked for the complete withdrawal of Russian forces from Afghanistan by February 1989. A non-aggression, non-intervention clause with Pakistan was also included in this agreement (obviously it was never implemented as ISI continued to meddle in Afghan affairs and is still heavily involved). It was also resolved that the refugees be repatriated honorably. The Geneva Accord proved to be a major victory for the US and General Zia as the Russians were defeated and their dream of getting access to the "warm waters" was completely denied. The demise of the former USSR brought an end to the bipolar world and the United States appeared as the singular superpower dictating world affairs.

The Afghan war defeat also proved to be the last straw in the subsequent disintegration of the Russian empire. August 17, 1988 saw the departure of General Zia from the scene when his military plane exploded midair killing him and 17 other top brass military personnel. The theories of his killing are numerous and uncorroborated. The air disaster also killed the US ambassador to Pakistan who was accompanying General Zia. Pakistan reverted back to some form of democracy and a series of short term civilian governments took over between 1990 and 2000 when another Army General (Pervez Musharraf) staged a successful coup. Pakistan has seen a decadal cycle of alternating military and civilian rules in its 66 years checkered history.

A USMC Captain told me a story about how he almost lost his wedding ring to an Afghan elder. "An Afghan asked me to see my wedding ring, I took it off and put it in his hands; he started walking away! I said no, this is a symbol of my wife's love so give it back. He started running away with it. I pulled my knife and threated him if he does not give it back I will have to stab him. Only then I got my ring back. We have given them so much, but the Afghans don't understand it and don't appreciate it".

Chapter 4
POST-SOVIET AFGHANISTAN

THE *MUJAHIDEEN* TUG OF WAR
1990-1996

With the departure of the Soviet troops, the communist government in Kabul was rendered weak and the *Mujahideen* stepped up their march to regain their country. *Mujahideen* captured one major town after another and continued their march toward Kabul. In 1990, General Abdul Rashid Dostum, a close ally of the communist government, abandoned the Kabul regime and established its own stronghold in Mazar-i-Sharif (Mazar-e-Sharif). Traditionally, the only time Afghans are united is when they find a common enemy. Once the threat is neutralized, the Afghans revert back to inter-tribal and ethnic warfare.

Meanwhile, Pakistan re-doubled its efforts to establish a *Mujahideen* led government and Sibghatullah Mojaddadi was chosen as the leader of the new soon-to-be Afghan government. However, he was not acceptable to the liberal leaders of Kabul.

The interim government led by Mojaddadi never assumed power in Kabul. The communist government of Najibullah fell in 1992 as *Mujahideen* advanced towards Kabul. Elections were held in 1993 and Burhanuddin Rabbani was elected as the president of the new Afghan government. Civil war broke out in Kabul and northern leaders such as Abdul Rashid Dostum, Ahmad Shah Massoud and Gulbuddin Hekmatyar began to fight for control of Kabul. In-fighting intensified in the next two years and local warlords assumed more power. This is the time period when infrastructure in Afghanistan was damaged the most as every military leader resorted to using maximum fire power. There was no dearth of weapons and ammunition. Afghanistan remained without any effective central leader since the fall of the communist government in 1992. Consequently, a power vacuum was created. The Afghan people were getting exhausted of the constant bloodshed since 1980 and wanted a relative peace and quiet; another corollary of tribal life where the tribes want to take rest and re-energize and re-group.

RISE AND FALL OF TALIBAN
1996-2001

The local warlords became powerful and got a free hand to act at will. In one incident, a local warlord in Kandahar kidnapped two young girls and repeatedly raped them. *Mullah* Omar, along with 30 of his madrassa students (called Taliban in Pashto), freed the girls and hanged the warlord from the gun barrel of a tank; tribal-style justice was served. The news of this incident spread like a jungle fire and *Mullah* Omar became a household name overnight. The people of Kandahar and adjoining areas chose Omar as their spiritual and military leader (Supreme Commander) in 1994 and he assumed the title of Amirul Momineen (Commander of the faithful Muslims). People found a new Messiah in the form of *Mullah* Omar and local population started to flock towards him. Omar began to disarm the local leaders and brought more areas under his control. His popularity grew exponentially with every passing day. Omar knew the importance of capturing Kabul and started marching toward the capital once he gathered a sizeable militia.

Omar and his Taliban followers stormed Kabul and took over the government in 1996. Najibullah was hanged in the main square and his body was dragged in the streets of Kabul by the victorious Taliban. The official name of the country was once again changed and was now called the Islamic Emirates of Afghanistan. The Taliban ruled the country until late 2001 with an iron hand and it came to be known as the darkest period of recent Afghan history. Omar remained the de facto leader of the Kabul regime but stayed mostly in his stronghold of Kandahar and appeared very little in public. This was a pure theocracy and *Mullah*s were appointed to all government ministries. Taliban established swift justice centers and law and order was established immediately. Public hangings and other forms of archaic punishments were introduced and for a brief moment all illegal drugs such as opium poppy and hashish were banned.

All public appearance of women was banned and they were only allowed to work in education and medicine. There is a long history of Taliban antagonism towards women and it is partly related to their upbringing in Pakistani refugee camps and madrassas elsewhere, away from any women folk. The local Taliban commanders soon resorted to tyrannical ways to control the population and the locals started to revolt against them. Towards the end of Taliban rule in early 2000s, the general public was ready for another change.

Pakistan, UAE and Saudi Arabia were the only three countries which recognized the Taliban government in Kabul. The north in general remained skeptic of Kabul policies as women remained the prime target of Taliban brutalities. Initially, ISI hesitated from supporting Taliban, but as the movement gained momentum, ISI initiated contacts with Taliban leaders and started to patronize them. In 1998, the anti-Taliban leaders such as Rashid Dostum, Hekmatyar, Ahmad Shah Massoud and Rabbani put together a front called the Northern Alliance. The group was actively supported by Russia and had a one-point agenda; to oust the Taliban regime. Assassination of Ahmad Shah Massoud just two days before 9/11 was a big blow to the Northern Alliance.

OBL continued to support the Taliban regime both militarily and financially and established his global jihadist organization called Al-Qaeda (an Arabic word meaning "the base/foundation"). Al-Qaeda stood for destroying the West and establishing a global Islamic Caliphate system. Al-Qaeda recruited disgruntled elements from all neighboring Muslim countries including Egypt, Saudi Arabia, Yemen, Somalia, Pakistan and the Central Asian States. Al-Qaeda became not only active in Afghanistan but it also sent its men to Kashmir and Chechnya. The true Axis of Evil was evolving here in Afghanistan; the interests of Taliban, Al-Qaeda and ISI have finally converged. ISI proved to be a binding force between Taliban and Al-Qaeda and fully backed the repressive regime at Kabul. Financial support was provided by Bin Laden, manpower was provided by Taliban, while professional expertise was the responsibility of ISI.

The long association between ISI, CIA and OBL was about to be dismantled. By 1996, ISI was fully behind all Taliban activities and

CIA was displeased with it. After the defeat of the Red Army, OBL was all set to defeat the "other" enemy of Islam, i.e., the West. Al-Qaeda was getting stronger and no one was paying attention to its covert and overt evil designs. Jihadist organizations throughout the world were either pledging their allegiance to Al-Qaeda, or were highly inspired by its global philosophy. The US embassies bombings in Tanzania and Kenya on August 07, 1998 brought the names of the Al-Qaeda leaders to the forefront. OBL and Aiman Alzawahiri became household names overnight for completely different reasons in the West and in the Islamic worlds.

Since the Soviets departed the scene, the *Mujahideen* slowly transformed into Taliban and at the same time other terrorists were created. At present, it is hard to control the situation in a region where several powerful players have met their ultimate demise. Saudis, Iranians, Indians, afghans, central Asians, Pakistanis, Chinese, Americans, Israelis and Russians, all have gathered in one tiny place around the Khyber Pass to battle out their proxies. Taliban and other fundamentalists are the current owners of Islam; it remains unclear as to who will be the ultimate winners and losers this time around!

Chapter 5
THE AFGHAN SOCIETY

ETHNO-LINGUISTIC GROUPS

Pashtuns, Tajiks, Uzbeks, Hazara and Aimak constitute 90% of Afghan population (figure 4). Their relative proportions are uncertain and differ depending on whom you ask. If asked in the south where Pashtuns dominate, their relative proportion is 70% but this number can be as low as 35% if asked in the north where Tajiks and Uzbeks dominate. Hazara is a distinct ethnic group in the center of the country; practicing Shia religion and speaking their own language. Baluchis, Nuristanis, Turkmen, Pamiris, and Kyrgyz all together constitute about 10% of the population.

There has never been a completed census in Afghanistan. The one in 1979 could not be completed because of the Russian invasion and the one in 2001 remained unfinished because of the American attack. It is highly uncertain as to what is the exact population of Afghanistan or the relative proportion of various ethnicities. United Nations has recently downgraded the Afghan population from 33 million to 31 million because of the wrong projections based on the 2001 partial consensus. Numbers don't really mean anything in Afghanistan; they are, at best, educated guesses. As an example, the percent population of Pashtuns (the largest ethnic group) various between 45% and 70% depending on who do you ask (Figure 4). This is not a precise map by any means but it closely resembles the current ethnic distribution. If you ask an older Afghan about his age, the answer will be "about 50 or 60"; that's a 17% margin of error in a number which in fact is as accurate as possible in any other country. Consequently, numbers and figures don't really mean anything in Afghanistan.

Almost all the ethnic groups within Afghanistan transcend the international borders into neighboring states. Pashtuns are disproportionately divided by the DL, though they occupy more territory in Afghanistan because of the sparse population density.

With nearly 60 million members spreading across the DL, the Pashtuns are divided into five major groups: Durrani, Ghilzai, Ghurghusht, Karlani, and Sarbani with a recorded history dating back to at least 2000 BC. These groups are further divided into tribes, clans and families with complex inter-tribal relations. Durranis and Ghilzais have a feudal history for several hundred years and the Taliban insurgency is a part of this inter-tribal feud.

Pashto and Dari are considered the official languages of Afghanistan, and are spoken by 85% of the people, though more emphasis is placed on Dari in official communication. Dari is also considered as the language of the 'civilized' segments of the society while Pashtu is more associated with war and tribalism. The Turkish languages, (especially Uzbek and Turkmen) are spoken primarily in the north by about 12% of the population. Several dozen other minor languages are also spoken in the country representing about 5% of the population. Bilingualism and multilingualism is common a large degree amongst the inhabitants of the country. Islam remains the official religion of Afghanistan and affects all aspects of Afghan life. About 95% of the population is Muslim with minor amounts of Sikhs, Hindus and Jews. Majority of the Muslims (about 84%) belong to the Sunni sect.

Loyalty to one's family and tribe remains a central tenant for each Pashtun member and is the primary reason that Pashtuns have not been subdued by an external force from Alexander the Great to NATO Allies. A Pashtun tribal elder told a visiting British officer in 1809, "We are content with discord, we are content with alarms, we are content with blood ...[but] we will never be content with a master" (Tanner, 2002). An unwritten code of *Pashtunwali* dictates the daily lives of all Pashtuns. It is an honor code which specifies roles for each member of a family, both male and female, with the head of the group wielding most powers and influence.

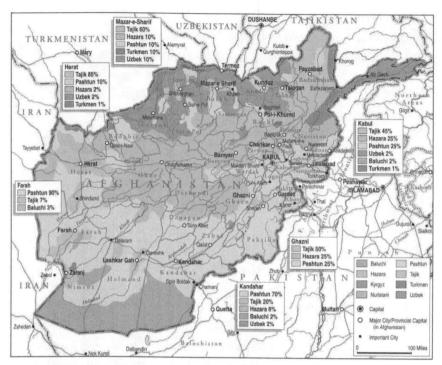

Figure 4: Ethno-linguistic subdivisions in Afghanistan and surrounding countries (From: ISW, 2009).

PASHTUNWALI

The unwritten code of Pashtuns is known as *Pashtunwali* which has been passed on to successive generations. It is applied to various degrees in the Pashtun society. This code has been handed down to Pashtuns for their recorded history dating back to several thousand years. *Pashtunwali* is based on honor, respect, valor, hospitality, and Pashtun nationalism. In some cases it is in direct conflict with Sharia laws and the legal framework applied on both sides of the DL. *Pashtunwali* is an integral part of Pashtun identity. "By adhering to *Pashtunwali* a Pashtun possesses honor (*izzat*); without honor s/he is no longer considered a Pashtun, and is not given the rights, protection, and support of the Pashtun community" (Kakar, 2004).

When a Canadian Army Lieutenant was hit by an Afghan with an axe shouting Allah-o-Akbar, the Canadians were stunned "hindered by a limited understanding of the term, many assumed that the tenets of *Pashtunwali* were universal and accepted by all Afghans; sadly this was not the case" (Strickland, 2007). John C. Griffiths (2001) cited historian Mountstuart Elphinstone describing Pashtuns in 1808 as "Their vices are revenge, envy, avarice, rapacity and obstinacy; on the other hand, they are fond of liberty, faithful to their friends, kind to their dependents, hospitable, brave, hardy, frugal, laborious and prudent; they are less disposed than the nations of their neighborhood to falsehood, intrigue and deceit".

Stephen Tanner (2002) cited the poetry of Khushal Khan Khattak, one of the greatest poets of Pashto language who lived in the 17th century and fought against the Mughals, as;

"Glory's the hazard, O man of woman born!
The very name Pakhtun spells honor and glory
Lacking that honor what is the Afghan story?
In the sword alone lies our deliverance".

Recent writers and intellectuals have questioned the tenants of *Pashtunwali* and asked for reforms. Qudratullah Hadad believes that a Pashtun cannot become a member of the Pashtun family just by blood; rather s/he must earn it by service to the community. Rana Momand believes that "If I had to remove a few rules of Pashtunwali, they will be "*gherat*" (honor) and "*badal*" (revenge). I think these two elements have an immense power in distracting so many Pashtuns".

Pashtuns and their honor code have faced many challenges over time. From Syed Ahmed (1820s), to Abdullah Azzam and OBL (1980s) to the present day Taliban are all busy bringing the "ignorant Muslims" back to the "right" path of the Salaf-e-Saliheen (the original Islam imposed 1400 years ago). Thus, the present attempt can be viewed as a genuine, internal struggle from the heart of Islam to the rest of the Muslim world to create a Muslim Ummah (Muslim Nation). Pashtuns have always resisted foreign influences and dominance and therefore have been viewed as being problematic and a hindrance to the invaders. Pashtuns have in general refused to change their traditional customs after conversion to Islam has always been an irritation in the eyes of the Wahabis. Wahabis are trying to rid Pashtuns of their cultural heritage. Money pouring from Saudi Arabia and Qatar is spent on building mosques and madrassas all over Pakistan and Afghanistan. Saudis are providing all the expenses for these structures along with salaries for the employees, free books and tuition money.

Burki (2011) commented on the Wahabi influence as follows; "…… the overwhelming majority of Pashtuns continued to adhere to their pre-Islamic traditions and to their tribal lineages. Furthermore, the average Pashtun did not buy the Muslim "brother" line; rather, they proudly identified with their clan and then with their tribe. Pashtun xenophobia has not excluded Muslims and frequently has even included other Pashtuns who were not closely related. Even more egregious in the eyes of the Wahhabis, some of these "Muslim" brothers stubbornly retained an ancient narrative of being *Bani Israel* as a source of pride of lineage, much to the Wahhabis disgust".

The Taliban, with the financial backing and support of OBL, sought to implement Sharia and to ban *Jirga*s (an essential mechanism of *Pashtunwali*). They were not very successful in their efforts, however, they have started to substitute Arabic words for Pashto lexicon with some success over time. The use of *'Jirga'* was officially replaced by the term *'shura' which stands for* 'council' in Arabic. Pashto greetings have largely been discouraged and replaced with Arabic greetings. Similarly, baby names have now been replaced with pure Arab names.

Unfortunately, the indiscriminate bombing of the atheist Red Army eventually paved the way for the Wahabi/Deobandi influences to creep into the Pashtun society. The Pashtun tribal structures were gradually weekend and extensive population dislocation in Afghanistan eventually led to a failed state. This factor alone facilitated the Taliban takeover of Afghanistan in 1996 more than anything else. The Omar-led Taliban are sympathetic to Wahabis because of similar ideologies and interests in Afghanistan and therefore granting guest status to OBL and Alzawahiri was hardly a surprise to the local analysts.

"We have preconceived notions about the nature of the insurgency that may be misguided or even false. We have a deeply flawed understanding of the Pashtun people and *Pashtunwali*, the way of the Pashtun. We do not understand the roles and importance of the tribes and elders, the influence of the *Mullahs* and Islam, or the competition for power among the tribes, Islam, and the government (Malevich and Youngman, 2011)".

The net effect of all these "foreign" influences is that Pashtuns are losing their identity and foreigners have started to feel it. "We were not seeing the fiercely independent and aggressive Afghan. Could this really be the 'Graveyard of Empires'? We were not seeing great men of honor. Could this really be the land of *Pashtunwali*—the unwritten code of conduct that places such an emphasis on honor?" (Goepner, 2012).

Chapter 6
REGIONAL PLAYERS

The geographic location of Afghanistan has always played a pivotal role in the events happening inside the country. The regional powers of today and in the past have always viewed it a cross-roads and invaders have never hesitated to use it a proxy battlefield. Of all the neighbors surrounding Afghanistan, only a few have played an active role in the relative stability or lack thereof inside the country. Russia, Pakistan, Iran, CARs and India have taken keen interest in the internal affairs of Afghanistan while Saudi Arabia, Qatar and UAE have funneled their money directly or through proxies. USA, as the sole super power, has remained deeply entrenched in Afghanistan since dislodging the Taliban in 2011. China has remained a silent spectator and recently started to take interest in the natural resources of Afghanistan. "Afghanistan's neighbors – including China, Iran, Tajikistan, Turkmenistan and Uzbekistan – all have legitimate interests in the country and its long-running conflicts. Many other states, including India and Russia, also have legitimate interests in whether Afghanistan can manage to stay together, make progress in development, and attract refugees back" (Roberts, 2009).

PAKISTAN

The recent general elections of 2013 indicate an extreme fragmentation of the individual components (Provinces) in the country. Punjab has overwhelmingly elected its own nationalist leaders, while Khyber Pukhtunkhwa (the Province adjoining Afghanistan formerly known as NWFP) has elected to power a coalition of right-wing religious parties led by former cricket star Imran Khan and his party, PTI (Pakistan *Tehreek-e-Insaf*). The PTI-led coalition has a soft spot for Taliban and is currently in the process of establishing contacts with the Taliban leaders to jump start a peace process. Based on examples from the past, the future of such talks remains doubtful.

Pakistan was originally carved out of India as an establishment for Indian elites. M. A. Jinnah (the founder of Pakistan) and his Muslim League was an elite group as compared to Indian National Congress which truly represented ordinary Indians. Today, Pakistan is being ruled by the same Elites in the form of inept bureaucrats, manipulative military junta, corrupt politicians and religious zealots. These elites have defaced the country to the extent that it has become a joke at the international scene. The people of Pakistan are equally to be blamed for this fiasco. They have been reluctant to embrace modern education and criticized the use of science and technology.

The decadal cycle of military and civilian governments in the past 67 years has hindered a real democratic process in Pakistan. Of the three branches of military in Pakistan, Army is the largest and strongest, the Air Force and Navy play a less significant role in Pakistan politics. So far Army was considered as a state within the state but recently analysts believe that Army has its own country called Pakistan. Political institutions were never allowed to flourish; rather personalities remained at the helm of affairs. The security situation has worsened since the US invasion of Afghanistan in 2001. Suicide bombings, roadside bombings, ransoms and target killings are the norm rather than the exception. People have started not to care because after every turn of events, they adapt themselves to what is called the "new normal". After every suicide bombing, people get more lethargic and turn their faces away, as if it is business as usual. In the past 15 years, the country been fortified and barricaded and further buried under rubble, no pun intended!

To many analysts, Pakistan has only ONE problem; population explosion! It is now almost 200 million, that is just mind boggling for a country slightly more than the size of Texas. Analyze any problem in Pakistan and it can be traced to an unhindered increase in birth rate in the country. Terrorism has virtually eliminated the remaining sources of entertainment. There is a huge uprising in Baluchistan Province. Political killings and disappearances are on the rise. Nawab Akbar Bugti, a Baluch nationalist leader, was brutally murdered in 1996 along with his fellows while he was hiding in a cave after being chased by Pakistan Army.

Pakistan has a complex relationship with Afghanistan and it has contributed the most to Afghanistan's ongoing woes. There has been a "Pakistan connection" in all the wars in Afghanistan since the Soviet intervention in 1979. ISI had played a major role in controlling various Afghan factions. ISI's role has not always been under the control of civilian governments in Pakistan. During the 1980s, the western powers used ISI as its major channel to fund the war against the Russians in Afghanistan. Pakistan installed the

Taliban and officially supported the Taliban government from 1996 to 2001. The current Taliban insurgency against CF is largely controlled from Pakistan and ISI is once again playing a crucial role. Taliban recruits are replenished from madrassas across the border in Pakistan. These sanctuaries will remain in effect in the foreseeable future as Pashtuns inhabit the region across the DL. There is a lack of foresight in the US policy towards Pakistan as to how to deal with cross-border terrorism.

According to Roberts (2009) "The fact that Washington considers the Pakistani authorities unreliable, with certain elements willing to pass on intelligence to America's enemies, means that the US military role on the territory of Pakistan cannot be based on close military cooperation. As a result, US military action in Pakistan is bound to be perceived as an infringement of Pakistan's sovereignty". President George W. Bush issued an order in July 2008 which authorized the use of force in Pakistan without seeking the approval of the Pakistani government. The use of drone strikes has inflicted a significant dent on the operations of Al-Qaeda and Taliban in the border region while irking a reaction from the Pakistani establishment and general public. Pakistani leaders have publically condemned the drone strikes. The most valuable operation was conducted by the US Seal Team 6 that resulted in the death of OBL on May 02, 2011.

IRAN

Shia population in the Hazarajat region, and river water distribution are the main reasons for Iranian involvement in Afghanistan. Iran benefits from its involvement in Afghanistan in several ways; firstly, Iran supports Shia population in Afghanistan and promotes Shia religion outside of its borders; secondly, water from Amu River (Amu Darya) in north and Helmand River in the south end up in Iran. In fact Amu River serves as a 300 mile long international boundary with Iran. Third and most importantly, Iran wants to exert its leverage in order to remain a regional power. Iran also wants an uninterrupted water supply to its farmlands in the eastern part of the country. Currently, Afghans are not properly utilizing their water resources and Iran fears that if Afghans dam the river waters, Iran will not receive as much water as they are presently receiving. There are still millions of Afghan refugees living in Iran and it has been a source of tension between the two countries.

INDIA

Afghans have kept Indians close to their hearts and that alone is enough to make Pakistanis uncomfortable. Much has been covered about Indian interests in Afghanistan in the section on Pakistan but suffice is to say that India is ready to bring down Pakistan while at the same eyeing to get a fair share of Afghan riches. India does not share a direct border with Afghanistan but the two have always viewed each other as neighbors. India has established a large number of consulates along the DL and is a major contributor in the Afghan reconstruction effort. Salma dam in Herat Province and the new parliament house in Kabul are two major projects India is currently funding. India is also heavily investing in developing the Information Technology sector in Afghanistan. Some Afghans view India's increased involvement with a jaundiced eye as it might lead to a further escalation of tension between India and Pakistan.

CENTRAL ASIAN REPUBLICS (CARs)

Central Asian Republics of Turkmenistan, Uzbekistan and Tajikistan share common boundaries and history with Afghanistan. Ethnic groups from these three CARs frequently cross border into Afghanistan for social, cultural and economic reasons. Turkmenistan, Afghanistan, Pakistan and India are part of the Trans-Afghanistan pipeline which will transport natural gas from the Caspian Sea to these countries. Some analysts believe that this project is a major factor in the continued warfare in Afghanistan. Multiple factors have hindered the completion of this project that has been partly funded by Asian Development Bank. Uzbekistan and Tajikistan have significant ethnic populations in Afghanistan but those borders are not as porous as the DL. River water distribution can become a thorny issue if Afghanistan decides to build dams on Amu River in northwestern part of the country.

CHINA

The rivalry between India and Pakistan has played well for their northern neighbor. China has fully exploited this situation and remained a close friend and ally of Pakistan since 1947. China and India are not only economic rivals but they also have unresolved border issues. China has remained on the sidelines as for as the kinetics of the Afghan conflict are concerned. Its only interest is in the mineral resources of the country and it has already started bidding on some of the mine leases in Afghanistan.

RUSSIA

Russia has been on the losing end of the Afghan conflict since the disintegration of its predecessor USSR after its troops pulled out in 1988. Russia inherited this conflict and it cannot remain detached from something in its immediate neighborhood. Russia would be content with disengagement from Afghanistan if NATO completes its pull out in 2014. "Afghanistan's long-term prospects for political stability and economic prosperity depend on strengthening its links with these neighbors. Both the Afghan government and the international community therefore must give far greater attention to the structure of these relationships, their present status, and their future prospects when creating development and security policies for Afghanistan" (AIAS, 2008)

Gulab Mengal, former Governor of Helmand, summarized the role of regional countries as follows; "If we are sitting in a room and I got a problem with you and I ask you to take it outside. For these regional players, that "outside" is Afghanistan". Those countries interfere the most in Afghanistan who benefit the most from it. "All neighboring countries interfere in Afghanistan from Turkmenistan to China in the north, however, the governments of Pakistan and Iran have the most hand in Afghanistan affairs" said Abdul Qauym, Deputy Governor of Now Zad District in Helmand Province. "Let it be very clear that we are not against the peoples of these two countries; it's their governments which are creating problems for us. Similarly, Iranians are promoting their Shia religion not only in Afghanistan but throughout the world as well" he further said.

PART II
MINERAL AND WATER RESOURCES

Chapter 7 Geology and Politics
Afghan Geo-Politics
Geology of Afghanistan

Chapter 8 Mineral Resources
Rare Earth Minerals
Heavy Metals
Industrial Minerals
Energy Resources
Gemstones
Challenges

Chapter 9 Water Resources
Surface Water
Kajaki Dam
Salma Dam
Ground Water

Chapter 10 Population and Resource Wars

Chapter 7
GEOLOGY AND POLITICS

AFGHAN GEO-POLITICS

"An internal Pentagon memo states that Afghanistan could become the 'Saudi Arabia of lithium', a key raw material in the manufacture of batteries for laptops and BlackBerrys" New York Times, June 13, 2010.

The term 'geo-politics' assumes a new meaning when viewed in the Afghan context. Alexander 'The Great' wandered into this territory in 4th century BC. Mughals swept through the Khyber Pass to invade and conquer India. The British were defeated several times before settling the borders with Afghanistan in the

19th century. The Russians ventured and ultimately reached their strategic and geographic death on the Afghan soil, and lately the Americans are scratching their heads as to what is it that they want from their misadventure. Whether it's the Britons controlling the unruly Afghan tribes or the Russians trying to access the 'Indian Ocean warm waters' or the Americans trying to intimidate the Chinese, the Afghan soil possesses some strange ingredient to which all great civilizations are attracted.

I believe we have finally come to an agreement regarding the nature of this centripetal force commonly known as 'the Afghan soil'. The Russians and French knew it in early 20th century that the Afghan soil is rich in mineral resources. They extensively mapped the terrain and trained the Afghans on how to extract the mineral wealth. The process was halted in late 1970s as a result of the Russian invasion and subsequent destabilization of successive Afghan governments.

The technological advancements in the late 20th century have once again shifted the focus to the 'Afghan soil' as large deposits of Lithium, Uranium and Rare Earth Minerals have been confirmed by the US Geological Survey. Are we witnessing another phase of perpetual destabilization in Afghanistan? We will get a definitive answer in the near future.

GEOLOGY OF AFGHANISTAN

Just like its varied ethnic composition, the geology of Afghanistan is varied and complex. Mountains in the north and center were developed during the Alpine orogeny. Tectonic elements comprising today's Afghanistan come from 4 or 5 blocks at the leading edge of the Indian plate (Precambrian) and back end of the Asian block (Hercynides). The oldest rocks are Achaean (granites and gneisses) with a younging succession of rocks from the Proterozoic and every Phanerozoic system (sandstones and limestones) up to late Quaternary deposits (Figure 5). Molassic deposits occur at the foothills of Hindu Kush which is the major mountain range in the country (a western extension of the Himalayas). Orogenic processes are still going on as evidenced by seismic activity in the eastern part of the Hindu Kush and its foothills (Figure 6); Kabul lies in a most active seismic zone and therefore is prone to major seismic events.

This diverse geological setup has resulted in a significant mineral base with over 1400 mineral occurrences recorded so far. Mining history in the country started with precious stones such as lapis lazuli and emerald while at the same time artisanal mining of gold and copper commenced which continues till the present day. It is believed that some of the oldest known mines in the world have been established in Afghanistan to produce lapis lazuli for the Egyptian Pharaohs. The French and Russians conducted large scale geologic surveys in the 1960s and 70s which resulted in the discovery of significant resources of metallic minerals, including copper, iron, chromium, lead, zinc and gold, and non-metallics such as halite, marble, talc, gypsum, barite, beryl and mica (Figure 7). The bedrock geology of Afghanistan can be thought of as a jigsaw of crustal blocks separated by fault zones, each with a different geological history and mineral prospection (Figure 8). This jigsaw has been put together by a series of tectonic events dating from the Jurassic. The tectonic compression zone, formed with formation of Himalayas, created many natural gas pockets mostly in Jurassic, and some in the Cretaceous period. The tectonic compression zone also led to the formation of a few oil traps in Neogene and Paleogene beds which are stable since Mesozoic (Figure 9).

The USGS has re-interpreted much of the Afghan geology and is available on its website. Geologic studies were previously conducted by the Russians and French. USSR geoscientists did not accept plate tectonics as a viable concept and believed in the concept of Depositional Basins.

Era	Period		Epoch	Age (Ma)
Cenozoic	Quaternary Modern humans		Holocene	0.01
			Pleistocene	
				2
	Tertiary Mammals diversify; early hominids	Neogene	Pliocene	5
			Miocene	23
		Paleogene	Oligocene	34
			Eocene	55
			Paleocene	65
Mesozoic	Cretaceous	Flowering plants common; major extinction including dinosaurs & ammonoids		
				144
	Jurassic	Early birds & mammals; abundant dinosaurs		
				206
	Triassic	Abundant coniferous trees; first dinosaurs; first mammals		
				250
Paleozoic	Permian	Mass extinction of many marine animals including trilobites		
				290
	Carboniferous Fern forests; insects; first reptiles; crinoids; sharks; large primitive trees		Pennsylvanian	314
			Mississippian	360
	Devonian	Early tetrapods, ammonoids, & trees		409
	Silurian	Early land plants & animals		439
	Ordovician	Early Fish		500
	Cambrian	Abundant marine invertebrates; trilobites dominant		540
"Precambrian"	Proterozoic	Single-celled and, later, multi-celled, soft-bodied organisms; first invertebrates		
				2,500
	Archean	Oldest fossils: bacteria & other single-celled organisms		
		Oldest known fossils		3,800

Figure 5: Geologic Time Scale with ages given in millions of years.

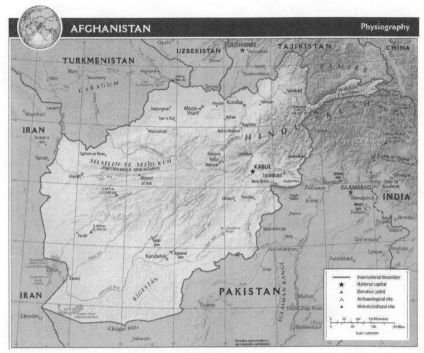
Figure 6: Physiography of Afghanistan.

Figure 7: Afghan mineral development projects (From: Randall and Owen, 2012).

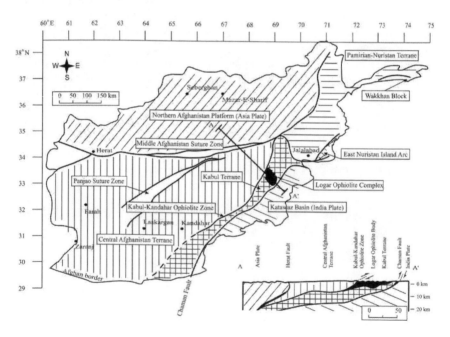

Figure 8: Simplified tectonic map of Afghanistan showing various terranes and the Logar Ophiolite Complex (From: Benham et al., 2009).

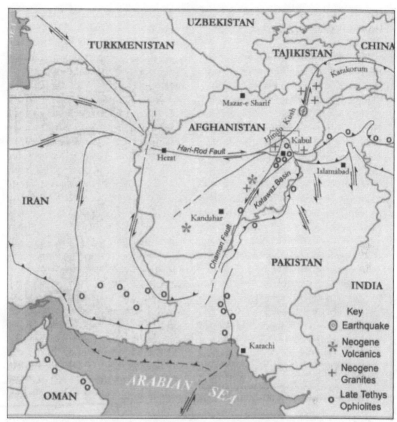

Figure 9: Tectonic elements in the Afghan Block.

Chapter 8
MINERAL RESOURCES

Afghanistan has a wide range of largely untapped mineral and energy resources: copper, iron, gold, uranium, cobalt, mercury, cesium, marble, and a number of minerals containing rare earth elements. Large deposits of niobium (used in steel making), and molybdenum which can withstand high temperatures and is used in making various alloys are also present. Recent studies indicate that Afghanistan is home to valuable deposits of lithium (used in batteries to run electronics). A Pentagon official once described Afghanistan as "the Saudi Arabia of lithium". Large deposits of industrial minerals and energy resources are waiting to be explored and exploited.

RARE EARTH MINERALS

Rare Earth Elements (REEs) are those chemical elements on the periodic table represented by lanthanides with atomic numbers (Z) 57 through 71. In order of increasing atomic number, REEs are lanthanum (La), cerium (Ce), praseodymium (Pr), neodymium (Nd), promethium (Pm), samarium (Sm), europium (Eu), gadolinium (Gd), terbium (Tb), dysprosium (Dy), holmium (Ho), erbium (Er), thulium (Tm), ytterbium (Yb) and lutetium (Lu). Scandium (Z 21), and yttrium (Z 39) are not REEs, but generally grouped with the lanthanides because they have similar physical and chemical properties and can be found within the same geologic formations. REEs are all metallic elements closely related to each other in their chemical properties, geochemical coherence and distribution in the earth's crust. Minor amounts of Thorium and Uranium always occur associated with the REE minerals (Sukumaran, 2012).

The term *rare earth* is a misnomer as these elements are not rare at all, being found in low concentrations throughout the Earth's crust and in higher concentrations in certain minerals. REEs can be found in almost all massive rock formations. However, their concentrations range from ten to a few hundred parts per million by weight. Therefore, finding them where they can be economically mined and processed presents a challenge (Hurst, 2010). Rare earths are large-ion-lithophile elements (LILE) just like Uranium and Thorium that are incompatible in the structure of upper mantle minerals and are thus fractionated into the earth's crust. REEs are more abundant in the earth's crust as compared to Chromium, Nickel, Copper, and Zinc, but they do not form deposits of sufficient economic value. "Because of the dispersed nature of REE minerals in rocks, geological exploration to locate REE deposits is a daunting task" (Sukumaran, 2012).

REEs have been used in conducting geologic research especially petrogenesis; to trace the origin of rocks to determine if they were originated in the earth's crust or mantle. REEs are used in high-tech applications, including critical military-based technologies such as night-vision goggles and precision guided weapons. REEs are also used in key technologies that have been successfully applied to modern militaries such as lasers, fluorescents, permanent magnets, fiber optic communications, hydrogen energy storage, and superconducting materials. Non-military uses include LCD screens, MRI, rocket-space and aviation, microelectronics, and electrical engineering, positron emission tomography (PET), portable X-ray units, petroleum refining, and glass coloring (Hurst, 2010). The unique properties of REEs (nuclear, metallurgical, chemical, catalytic, electrical, magnetic and optical) make them indispensable and non-replaceable in these applications (Sukumaran, 2012).

China is currently the sole provider of REEs from the world's largest rare earth mine in Bayan Obo, China. According to USGS, Afghanistan sits on mineral resources worth 3 trillion USD. If properly explored, exploited and managed, this could possibly transform Afghanistan into a wealthy nation! China is already in the lead for bidding on some of the mineral resources, followed by India. Currently, China is in the forefront to mine these resources and they have signed various contracts with the Afghanistan government. USGS has been using satellite imageries and conducting remote-sensing data collection and on-the-ground fieldwork under military cover to verify old estimates and locate potential new deposits. The most promising site for REEs is located around a dead volcano near the village of Khan Nashin (also spelled Khanneshin) in southern Helmand (Figure 10). The volcano is located in the Registan Desert ~150 miles southwest of the city of Kandahar. Geologists believe that the volcano was formed during the early Quaternary period (~2.5 million years ago) through multiple episodes of carbonatite volcanism (Mars and Rowan, 2011). Carbonatite volcanism is rare in nature and is of economic value because of its association with REEs and Uranium and Thorium. ASTER (Advanced Spaceborne Thermal and Reflection Radiometer) data were used to identify carbonate rocks within the volcano.

So far USGS has mapped 1.3 million metric tons of the volcanic deposits and the Pentagon has estimated its value to be close to 100 billion USD. The Khan Nashin volcano was never studied in great detail; at least not from the REE exploration point of view. Prior to the USGS detailed studies, a U.S. Navy NP-3D aircraft from "Scientific Development Squadron One" flew over Afghanistan for three months and gathered geological data from the air (Figure 9). The aircraft flew mostly straight lines, spaced about 2.5 miles apart (Burgess, 2006). Geophysical instruments mounted on the aircraft measured earth's magnetism and other properties and the Naval Research Lab geophysicists generated three-dimensional views of the uppermost 6 miles of Afghanistan's bedrock

The future of this deposit depends on the possibility of improving ground situation, especially in the southern part of the country which is under heavy Taliban influence. "Any mining at the Khan Nashin volcano would probably still be years off, however. Afghanistan has little experience with heavy industry, no real railroads and hardly any electrical power in rural areas. Those challenges are not the problem, though: major mining companies are accustomed to pioneering undeveloped frontiers in remote parts of Indonesia, Chile and Australia, for example. The need for exceptional security against hostile forces is the potential deal breaker" (Simpson, 2011).

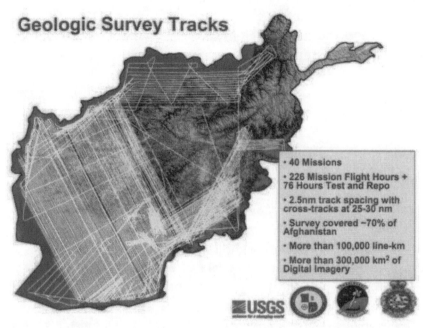

Figure 10: Results of aerial geophysical survey conducted by US Naval Research Lab (From: Burgess, 2006).

HEAVY METALS

Situation in northern half of the country is relatively stable and small scale mining operations can be carried out with the help of local militias and warlords. Those areas host untapped rock formations containing iron, copper, zinc, tin, gold and other metallic minerals worth hundreds of billions of dollars. Ministry of Mines (MoM) is responsible for exploration and exploitation of mineral resources in Afghanistan and it is currently working on leasing and bidding operations for these commodities. In 2007, China Metallurgical Group outbid four international investors for a lease to develop the Aynak copper deposit located just south of

Kabul (Figure 11). This is a massive copper deposit worth 43 billion USD over the life of the mine at today's high price. Developing an enormous copper processing facility will require a lot of power generation and rail road infrastructure. The winning group has agreed to build two power plants and a rail link connecting the mine with CARs. Prior to investing in the project, coal supplies must be located, assessed and graded for development.

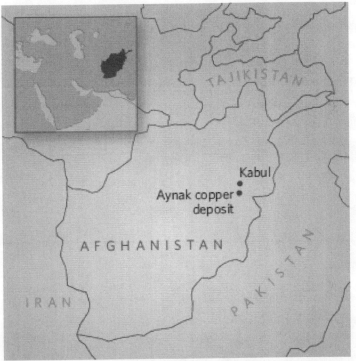

Figure 11: Location map of Ainak copper deposit.

In 1992, Chinese leader Deng Xiaoping said, "There is oil in the Middle East; there is rare earth in China." Seven years later, President Jiang Zemin wrote, "Improve the development and application of rare earth, and change the resource advantage into economic superiority". Leadership works!

The Haji-Gak iron ore (Fe) was discovered more than a century ago but Afghanistan has never had the right conditions and stability to start a major mining operation. The deposit is located in a mountainous terrain about 90 miles west of Kabul. According to MoM, it is estimated at 420 billion USD, the resource could bring in 300 million USD in government revenue each year and employ 30,000 people. Another prospective iron deposit is located in Furmorah District of Badakhshan Province which is a skarn deposit with associated phosphorous (P), sulfur (S), manganese (Mn) and nickel (Ni).

Gold (Au) is present both as lode deposits and placers along the river beds in Takhar and Ghazni Provinces. A number of gold bearing quartz veins have been identified in Badakhshan and adjacent Provinces. Lead (Pb) and zinc (Zn) deposits have been reported from Nalbandon (Ghor Province) and Spira (Paktia Province). The largest Pb-Zn deposit has been discovered from Darra-i-Nur and Kalai-Assad areas in Kandahar Province.

INDUSTRIAL MINERALS

Large amounts of marble, asbestos, barite, chromite, clays, gypsum, talc, manganese, graphite and halite have been reported in recent years and they have good prospects of supporting large scale industries. All these minerals are currently used in reconstruction efforts by international donors.

ENERGY RESOURCES

Oil exploration commenced in 1957 in Afghanistan. A number of oil and gas fields were discovered until 1984 when war effectively stopped all exploration activities. According to USGS, an estimated 1.6 billion barrels of crude, 15.7 trillion cubic feet of natural gas and 562 million barrels of natural gas liquids of undiscovered oil and gas resources are present in northern part of the country. In April 2011, MoM qualified several companies, including China's CNPC, UK's Tethys, Australia's Buccaneer Energy, Pakistan's Petroleum Exploration and Schlumberger to take part in an oil tender covering three blocks in the northern Amu Darya basin (Figure 12). Tethys Petroleum could be the first company to re-enter Afghanistan's upstream play since the war began in 1979 (Wan, 2011).

According to MoM, an estimated 80 million barrels of oil is present in the three blocks – Bazarkhami, Kashkari, and Zamarudsay – of the basin. "The Angot field, in Kashkari, is producing 800 barrels per day. Our modeling…… indicates we can produce 20,000 b/d in around 12-18 months for the discovered fields" said Tethys chief executive officer David Robson.

Figure 12: Amu Darya (River Amu) petroleum basin.

GEMSTONES

The principal gemstones of Afghanistan are lapis lazuli, emerald, ruby, sapphire, and spinel. Lesser known gems from the country include kunzite, aquamarine, spodumene, amethyst, tourmaline, morganite, and garnet. Almost all of the gem deposits are found in or near the Hindu Kush mountains in the northeast including Badakhshan, Kunar, Laghman, Kabul and Nangrahar Provinces.

The emerald mines are located in the famous Panjsher Valley leading out of the tall Hindu Kush and aiming at Kabul. The valley has been historically used by advancing and retreating armies to attack Kabul. Mining activity is still conducted on antiquated means and is very dangerous; mine safety has never been done on modern scientific lines. Emerald mineralization occurs in metamorphosed carbonate rocks. The India-Asia continental collision resulted in bringing chromium in deep-seated mafic rocks into contact with beryllium bearing crustal rocks. Later, alteration caused by hydrothermal fluids resulted in the formation of emeralds.

Considerable quantities of tourmaline (blue, pink and green in color) as well as significant amounts of kunzite and some aquamarine have been mined from the pegmatite veins in Nuristan Province. Smaller quantities of ruby, garnet, spinel, amethyst and morganite have been discovered in the Sarobi District of Kabul Province. Rubies and sapphires are found in steeply dipping marble beds east of Kabul at the towns of Jegdalek and Gandamak and have been mined for thousands of years. Lapis Lazuli is the most widely known mineral from Afghanistan. It is mined form marbles associated with high-grade metamorphic rocks in Badakhshan Province, northeast of the Panjsher Valley.

CHALLENGES

All the stakeholders involved in the Afghan mineral development are facing formidable challenges. There is a severe shortage of geoscience professional in the country. The few remaining professionals from the pre-Soviet invasion era are ill-equipped to use modern technologies currently used in mineral exploration. Four decades of science is "missing" in Afghanistan. There are just 100 Afghan professionals currently working in MoM headquarters in Kabul which has recently been renovated with 6.8 million USD of US taxpayers' money.

Security concerns sums up the fears of all international stakeholders, especially the westerners. Researchers conducted field work on the Khan Nashin volcano under heavy air and ground security provided by USMC. "These resources are not worth anything if you can't get there or don't have enough security to get them out of the ground" said Stan Coats, former principal geologist for the British Geological Survey. MoM Licensing regulations add to the uncertainty by requiring exploration companies to register their findings with the government, which then puts the resources out to bid. "You are not going to see a lot of Western interest in going out to expend scarce exploration dollars just to be outbid by the Chinese or someone else with more influence," says Jim Yeager, a U.S. consulting geologist who advised MoM on the 2007 tender of the 6 million-ton Aynak copper deposit. Randall and Owen (2012) described the situation as follows: "The money and blood pit that is Afghanistan – where the US and Britain have expended more than 2,100 lives and £302bn – is about to start paying a dividend. But it won't be going to the countries which have made this considerable sacrifice. The contracts to open up Afghanistan's mineral and fossil-fuel wealth, and to build the railways that will transport them out of the country, are being won or pursued by China, India, Iran, and Russia".

Even if all of the challenges are somehow overcome in the near-future, a lot of forethought has to be put in developing a large-scale mineral industry in Afghanistan for the simple reason of environmental degradation. Four decades of war has severely impacted the serene environment of the country. Hundreds of thousands of tons of ammunitions has been detonated by Afghans and international forces and there have been reports of the use of chemical weapons. Explosives have been constantly detonated on Camp Dwyer in southern Helmand. All trash produced on ISAF Bases has to be burnt leading to more air pollution (Photo 6).

Even some developed countries are still reeling from the adverse effects of open-pit mining and related environmental hazards. Simpson (2011) put it this way "Whether newly trained scientists and politicians can follow through with business development is unclear. Luckily, the rocks can wait. They have all the time in the world".

Photo 6: The ISAF requires any trash to be burnt on all of its bases.

Chapter 9
WATER RESOURCES

Just like other natural resources, water also falls under three governmental agencies; Afghanistan Geological Survey (AGS), Ministry of Mines (MoM) and Ministry of Energy and Water (MEW). Both surface and ground water resources are present throughout the country, but the south is more arid in general. Only 12 million of its total land area of 145 million acres is cultivable. Major portion of the arable land must be irrigated to produce crops.

Major rivers (Amu, Kabul, Helmand, Arghandab, Farah and Khash) are fed by glaciers and melting of fresh snow packs (Figure 12). Studies indicate that major glaciers in the Pamirs and Hindu Kush (Armstrong et al., 2010; Kaya, 2012; Sarkar, 2011; Scheel, 2009) are shrinking and thus the source for these rivers is drying up. A decrease in river water levels and higher, unregulated consumption is causing a decline in major wetlands. The Sistan wetland is a prime example of this decline and it is now almost dried up.

Very little data is currently available on water resources as most of the hydrologic and climatic data-collection activities were interrupted in the early 1980s. Aerial bombings and civil wars have destroyed many of the data collection facilities and for the most part historic record has been lost. Data collection was resumed in 2003 as USGS started collaboration with AGS. Stream flow data on some points is now available while efforts are being made to conduct ground water monitoring as well. Currently, sporadic ground water measurements are being carried out by USGS and AGS. It is believed that drinking water is at risk from open sewers and septic tanks.

SURFACE WATER

Helmand and Arghandab Rivers drain the southern part of the country and enter into Zabul Province in the eastern part of Iran. Western and southwestern parts of the country are irrigated by Murghap and Harirud rivers. The Afghan government established a water regulatory agency called HVA (Helmand Valley Authority) modeled after TVA (Tennessee Valley Authority) in the US. It was later expanded to HAVA (Helmand Arghandab Valley Authority). Thus HAVA is an added layer on the three governmental agencies already involved in controlling water resources in the country. On the ISAF side, the US Military's division of C-9 was responsible for coordinating and planning all developmental activities in southern Afghanistan and they were supported by professionals from USAID and USDA (Photo 7, 8).

Afghanistan has not promulgated a viable 'water law' so far. Inter-Province disputes are very common regarding the distribution of river waters. Helmand is considered a water bully in this regard; it is receiving more water from upstream Kandahar and releasing less water to downstream Nimroz; the river bed in Nimroz can sometimes be dry and locals cross it by foot. Wegerich (2010) described the Afghan water law as follows; "Overall, it appears that the sections within the law on permits and licenses are not implementable within or even useful for the traditional irrigation systems, but mainly play into the hands of the national hydrocracy and please international donors".

Photo 7: Officials from C-9, USAID, ISAF and Afghan Government are discussing strategy in the Water Summit at Camp Leatherneck, Helmand (February 2012).

Photo 8: The author presenting findings of his work at the Water Summit at Camp Leatherneck.

The majority of population in south and southwestern Afghanistan is located along the banks of these two rivers. As one moves away from the river valleys, vast deserts are encountered. The annual precipitation in the region is not more than 4 inches and 90% of which comes down in the months of February and March. All the major cities (Herat, Farah, Kandahar, Lashkar Gah, Gereshk, Musa Qala, Marjah and Zaranj) are built around the banks of these two rivers (Figure 13). The only major dam in southern Afghanistan is built on the Helmand River in the vicinity of Kajaki village. Salma Dam in western part of the country is currently under construction and is due to be completed by 2014.

Figure 13: Major regional River Systems (From Maps.com).

KAJAKI DAM

As part of the HVA, Kajaki dam was completed by the US in 1953. It is a concrete structure, 328 feet high and 890 feet long with an original storage capacity of 1.4 million acre-feet (Photos 9, 10). It is not precisely known as to how much of the reservoir has been silted up. The dam can produce up to 33 mega Watts of electricity. HAVA has met partial success in meeting its goals of irrigating the arid lands in Helmand and Kandahar Provinces. It has been heavily criticized for creating water logging and salinity conditions in the basin. Nick Cullather (2002) wrote in his epic article 'Damming Afghanistan; modernization in a buffer state' "It was lavishly funded by US foreign aid, multilateral loans, and the Afghan government, and it was the opposite of piecemeal. It was an "integrated" development scheme, with education, industry, agriculture, medicine, and marketing under a single controlling authority. Nation-building did not fail in Afghanistan for want of money, time, or imagination. In the Helmand Valley, the engines and dreams of modernization had run their full course, spooling out across the desert until they hit limits of physics, culture, and history".

Just like its past (Photo 11), the present also does not seem very promising. The dam site was heavily bombed by the British Air Force and has seen major battles between ISAF and Taliban/Chechen fighters in 2007. Parts of the dam have been restored by USAID since then.

The dam restoration project has been dubbed as the "Watershed of Waste" by the globalpost in its October 11, 2011 issue. The cost of the project has now climbed from 206 million in 2011 to 550 million USD (Huff Post, 2013). The project was initially slated for completion in 2005 and the new estimated date has been extended to 2015 with a number of lingering questions. The area is primarily controlled by Taliban and half-hearted efforts to clear the area have resulted in heavy casualties on the ISAF side. The project was characterized by globalpost as "The dam embodies USAID's unwieldy and corrupted Afghan development projects". The frustrated residents in the area are left with no other option but to rely on the expensive solar panels imported from China (Photos 12, 13).

Photo 9: Aerial view of Helmand River as it enters the Kajaki dam (June 2012).

Photo 10: The picturesque Kajaki reservoir as seen from an ISAF chopper (June 2012).

Photo 11: Hanging wires from an electric pole is a stark reminder of the Taliban hatred for civic amenities (November 2011).

Photo 12: Solar technology making inroads in rural Afghanistan (May 2012).

Photo 13: Solar panels for sale in a local bazar in Musa Qala (May 2012).

SALMA DAM

The earth and rockfill dam on the Harirud River is a manifestation of the increasing Indo-Afghan cooperation. It is 363 feet high and located 110 miles upstream of Herat city in Herat Province. The dam is crucial to the agro development of western parts of Afghanistan, however, its construction has created an uproar among the neighboring countries. Its construction has now been delayed by about 40 years as Iran is a downstream stakeholder. It can severely restrict the flow of water to Iranian border cities such as Mashhad. The 200 million USD project is paid for and engineered by India, and that is a problem for Pakistan. Afghan officials claim that they had thwarted a Taliban attack backed by ISI (Inter-Services Intelligence) in April 2013 to blow up the dam with heavy explosives (Peterson, 2013). If became operational in 2014, the dam will provide 44 Mega Watts of electricity and it will ease the Afghan dependency on Iran and Turkmenistan.

GROUND WATER

Drinking water is primarily supplied from ground water either through drilled or dug-wells. Drilled wells also constitute the only alternative source of irrigation water as well (Photos 14-16). Groundwater table has seen dramatic declines in the past three decades as recharge has decreased as a result of the global climate change. Dried dug-wells remind us of the shallow groundwater tables which have now declined to more than 120 feet below the land surface. Unregulated use of ground wand surface water is putting tremendous pressure on the water resources in the entire country. Non-Governmental Organizations such as DACAAR (Danish Committee for Aid to Afghan Refugees) helped the local communities in the past by providing drinking water through drilling a large number of drilled wells.

When the US military switched to the reconstruction process in 2008, there was no specific policy in place as to how to develop the water infrastructure. The battle space owners (Company and Battalion Commanders) used development of water infrastructure as a leverage to influence the local elders. More wells were drilled and more *Karezes* and canals were cleaned; all at a very high cost to the US taxpayers. In most cases, a very large number of wells were drilled in utter disregard of the local groundwater conditions. Consequently, the groundwater table in many areas of the country has gone dramatically down and most of the dug-wells are now reported as dry.

In one instance, a District Center of two miles across was punched with more than 300 water wells! For local contractors, well drillers and rig owners, it was a source of making easy money and a total wastage of the US taxpayers' dollars. Capt. Nixdorf, CAG team leader at Musa Qala (2011-12) asked me to check out a drilled well that was reported dry by the local DCOP. When I arrived at the scene, the DCOP had already arranged for a new contractor to drill a new well. He insisted that this well is dry and was not willing to let me check out the well. Finally, I was able to measure depth to water table and the well was so deep that eventually we ran out of the measurement line. The well had enough water to supply an entire village! The DCOP was not happy with my findings.

The irrigation system consists of two main mechanisms; the subterranean tunnels known as *Karez* (Photo 17) and drilled wells. The *karez* is a centuries-old system which is widely practiced in the entire region including the neighboring Baluchistan in Pakistan and several Iranian Provinces. This is a gravity driven system and water is distributed by a series of tunnels from higher elevation river sources to lower elevation crop fields and orchards. These *karezes* range in length from half a mile to four miles. *Karez* is a gravity-fed system and at the end of the tunnel water emerges in an open canal and the crops are irrigated through flood irrigation. The system requires minimal maintenance and is an effective method of minimizing water loss due to evaporation in a desert environment. The system has to be dug deeper as the region is going through a decade-long drought and an accompanying climate change. The system was also damaged during the British-led bombings of 2007-08. It also suffered because of a lack of maintenance during the past 40 years due to continued warfare. The *karez* system provided an effective mechanism for Taliban hideouts. These tunnels were used to move Taliban from one location to another without being detected. They were also used to transport large caches of arms and ammunitions. In some Districts under Taliban control, this system is still used for the same purpose.

Similarly, check dams and flood walls were erected solely to provide employment to the local population. The Dahana check dam in northern Helmand Province is a case in point (Photos 18-22). The local elders did not allow the building of a small dam because they wanted it to be 30 feet high on a stream with 4 feet peak discharge height. "Astonishment best describes my reaction to what I saw at Dahana", said GySgt Timothy A. Noller who served as the Assistant Team Leader for CAG. On the other hand, high-dollar projects were readily accepted by the local elders and Afghan government as it provided more employment opportunities and more money was changing hands. However, these high-dollar projects were put to no use; a famous situation arised when already clean *karezes* in Musa Qala District were cleaned again and again costing the US hundreds of thousands of dollars. Poor record keeping by BSOs and CAG Commanders resulted in duplication of contracts and the locals took full advantage of that. One such *karez* in the village of Khwaja Jamal was dry for 11 years but the locals managed to receive 5000 USD from the CERP funds to "clean" it again. The locals believed that by digging the *karezes* deeper would bring them more water. The issue is a rapidly falling ground water table as a result of unregulated water usage. The *karezes* have been heavily used by Taliban as hideouts and as a means of transportation of arms and ammo. A large portion of this money ends up in the hands of Taliban as they are close of relatives of the local contractors and other earning hands.

USAID awarded a 65 million USD project to IRD (International Relief & Development), a non-profit organization which specializes in international development and humanitarian assistance. The project worked under the title SRAD (Southern Regional Agricultural Development) aimed at developing water resource and agriculture infrastructure in southern Afghanistan SRAD was implemented in cooperation with the Ministry of

Agriculture, Irrigation and Livestock (MAIL) which has representatives at the District levels known as DAILs (Director of Agriculture, Irrigation and Livestock). Because of a lack of qualified personnel, the representatives at the District levels were either missing entirely or rarely reported to work. According to SRAD, its activities will (1) increase agri-sector jobs and incomes and (2) increase confidence of Afghans in their government, principally MAIL. They were hoping to achieve these goals through four tightly integrated objectives; cash for work, agro vouchers, training and capacity building and in-kind grants. In other words, SRAD was another step forward in running the welfare state in Afghanistan.

This money had to be spent in one year in two southern Provinces of Helmand and Kandahar. Craig (last name not disclosed) who served as the Agricultural Extension Specialist in Kandahar was worried because he was unable to find local avenues to spend his share of the money. Craig had to spend 180,000 USD on three greenhouses for which neither the expertise nor the materials were available. Craig was highly critical of the fact that he has been asked to give away a bag of carrot seeds to each farmer which was enough to grow carrots on an acre of land. If all of that seed had to be grown, it would have been enough to meet the carrot consumption of the entire Asian countries. 80% of the fertilizers and wheat seeds never made its way to the field and ended up in the local markets (Photo 23).

While presenting my findings to professionals of the Water Summit at Camp Leatherneck, I mentioned that Afghan officials were not available for duty and that led to the failure of some of the projects. USMC Col. Behseresht, OIC C-9, immediately called out a small meeting and said "Why did you put the Afghan officials on spot? Let's not do it for the rest of the day". So apparently we can't even mention the fact that Afghans should be present for duty in their OWN country! Earlier in the day I corrected an obvious error in the Colonel's presentation and that did not set well with him either; the Colonel was used to hearing "Yes Sir" only!

Photo 14: Diesel pumps discharge enormous amount of water depleting the aquifer at an alarming rate (Dahana, November 2011).

Photo 15: An Afghan child is filling in his water gallons with a hand pump from a drilled well.

Photo 16: The author measuring ground water quality and other physical parameters.

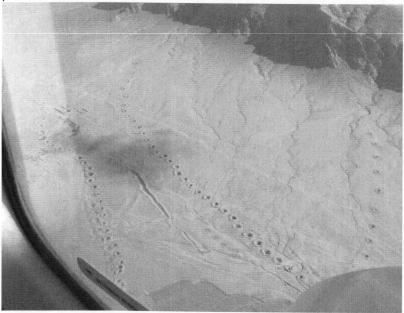

Photo 17: Aerial view of linear holes representing *karez* systems in northern Helmand. The holes are about 100 feet apart.

Photo 18: ISAF and DST officials trying to convince the locals to allow the construction of a check dam in Dahana.

Photo 19: The author is showing benefits of a check dam to the locals through the use of a physical model.

Photo 20: The author is inspecting the location for a check dam.

Photo 21: Mud cracks indicating desiccation in the stream bed close to the location of the proposed check dam.

Photo 22: The author is conducting field work on a dried stream bed in a tributary of the Helmand River.

Photo 23: Truckloads of wheat seed and fertilizer waiting to be distributed among the farmers of Kandahar Province.

Chapter 10
POPULATION AND RESOURCE WARS

As early as 1976, geologists predicted two contrasting scenarios for Afghanistan; it will either head towards large-scale development, OR internal chaos will prevail leading to an eventual loss of independence (Shroder, 1976). The latter situation is now a reality and the extraction and utilization of vast mineral resources now seems a distant reality.

The larger question one can ask is whether all of this conflict and chaos is driven by ethnic rivalries and regional and international politics or is there a "resource-driven" component to it as well? And if the answer is yes then what share goes to resources? To answer this question, we need to look elsewhere and analyze other conflict ridden regions of the world. A large number of variables can contribute to war, including but not limited to: population pressures, ethnic/tribal/racial hatred, conflicting ideologies, political repression, economic inequality, territorial ambitions, colonial expansion, psychological predilections, militarization, international alliances, destabilizing hegemony, and balance of power considerations (Sharp, 2007).

Angola, Congo, Rwanda, Nigeria, Sierra Leone, Darfur, Liberia, Peru, Kuwait, Columbia, Myanmar, Palestine, and Kashmir are just a few of the many examples where resources play a vital role in continuing the conflict over years and sometimes decades. States and non-state actors including criminal gangs are now vying for a wide range of natural resources including water, energy resources (coal, oil & gas) and minerals and gemstones. The causal mechanisms for conflicts and resources are not always clear but there is strong evidence that resource wealth has made conflicts more likely to occur, last longer and produces more casualties (Ross, 2004).

We are witnessing the emergence of an increasingly complex and volatile interplay of international and internal struggles over the control of natural resources. "On one side of this equation are the major powers — the United States, Russia, China, Japan, and Western Europe — that seek dominion over major resource-producing areas, such as the oil and natural gas fields of the Persian Gulf and Caspian Sea basins. On the other side are local factions — warlords, tribal chieftains, militia leaders, and so on — that aim to monopolize the revenues generated by particular resource deposits while enjoying the continued protection and support of their great-power patrons. The result, all too often, is the accelerated intrusion of arms, advisors, troops, and mercenaries into areas that are already bedeviled by internecine conflict" (Klare, 2007).

Competition to gain control of natural resources has led to widespread forced migrations and Afghans have seen some of the largest migrations in recorded history. Most of the migrants have permanently settled in either Pakistan or Iran and these two countries interfere the most in Afghanistan's internal affairs. "Humans themselves have become a commodity trafficked at great profit for asylum, labor, and/or sexual exploitation. Indeed, in 2001, the Australian government paid the island of Nauru--once rich in phosphates via strip mining--10 million USD to accept 300 Afghan asylum seekers rather than let them set foot on its Christmas Island territory" (Hein and Niazi, 2009).

The prospects of a large-scale mineral industry makes some Afghans worry about whether mining will be a good omen for their war-ravaged country. Mineral exploitation has recently been seen more as a curse rather than a blessing in many countries around the world. "The discovery of oil in Nigeria more than 50 years ago has earned billions of dollars for petroleum companies and the government, but most Nigerians still live on less than 1 USD a day. Development could fuel Taliban resurgence and government corruption" (Simpson, 2011). The resource curse argument states that "resource wealth, rather than benefiting a population, can in fact become a vice, when it encourages rent-seeking elites to establish a monopoly or oligopoly on resource exploitation making these elites independent from revenue through taxes and political support from the masses. Resource wealth thereby creates incentives and opportunities for insurgency as a means to monopolize resource rents through violence and war" (Korf, 2011).

Experts agree that natural resources alone cannot create a stable and secure environment. Strong institutions must be established first and only then mineral resources can be utilized to improve living conditions for ordinary citizens. If the country is weak, mineral resources become a curse and, therefore, Afghan mineral wealth will probably remain untapped in the foreseeable future. There is a strong need to start rebuilding the political institutions and civil society in Afghanistan so that mineral wealth can aid in making life better for the ordinary citizens.

PART III
PRESENT AND FUTURE

Chapter 11 The Insurgency
Greater American Involvement
Who Are Taliban?
Can Taliban Be Defeated?
Afghan War Asymmetry
The "Pakistan" Problem
The Poppy Culture

Chapter 12 The Afghan Government
Afghan National Security Forces
Afghan Corruption
GIRoA and Reintegration

Chapter 13 Development
Asymmetric Development
Women Development
Reconstruction and Development
Development and PRTs

Chapter 14 US/NATO Departure on the Horizon

Chapter 15 Missed Opportunities

Chapter 16 The Way Forward
American Legacy In Afghanistan
Regional Solution
The Elusive Future

Chapter 11
THE INSURGENCY

GREATER AMERICAN INVOLVEMENT

"We had a saying about the military in Afghanistan: the incompetent leading the unwilling to do the unnecessary".
Wright, Evan (2009).

The post 9/11 Afghanistan invited a wide array of players which added on to the ones who were already involved since 1979 when the then USSR invaded Afghanistan and installed a puppet government. The events of 9/11 changed the world forever and the word 'terrorism' assumed a new meaning. Osama Bin Laden (OBL) and his *Jihadi* terrorist organization 'Al-Qaeda' became the prime target of American military might in Afghanistan. OBL along with his Arab terrorists was hiding in Afghanistan after he was trained in Pakistan and fought against the former USSR on the Afghan soil. Because of Pakistan's heavy involvement in Afghanistan, US President George Bush asked Pakistani President General Pervez Musharraf in late 2001 "Are you with us or are you with them". Musharraf had no other option but to say YES and that's where the trouble started for Pakistani establishment.

Despite Musharraf's willingness to work with US on its war on terror, he could not fully control his own spy agency, the ISI (Inter-Services Intelligence). The Pakistani spy agency is headed by a General rank officer from the Army. Pakistani army works independently of the civilian government (if one is present) and ISI is even more independent so much so that its political wing determines which candidates will be elected and which party will be in power.

Competing agendas are in effect; the US and its allies are fighting the terrorists in Afghanistan and on the other hand ISI is supporting the Taliban in any possible way. The distrust between the US, its NATO allies and ISI started soon after the US invasion of Afghanistan in late 2001. Installing a friendly government in Kabul has always remained at the heart of the Pakistani administration and policy makers. Prior to the US invasion of 2001, Taliban were deemed as that friendly government which was seen as the most favored by Islamabad. Certain elements of ISI were getting increasingly Talibanized as the war progressed in Afghanistan. The Pakistan army eventually led an investigation into these allegations and a military court found five of its top officers having ties with terrorist organizations such as Hizbut Tehrir. They were convicted of overthrowing the government and creating a *Khilafah*. One of these convicts included a one-star General who was not only defiant in court but bragged about his ties to the terrorist organizations. Pakistan's history is full of military coups but this is the first time anyone has been tried and convicted of such a crime (Dawn News Report, 2011).

Pakistan controls the sea route to Afghanistan and therefore holds the key to any foreign military intervention in this country. The recent closure of the land route in 2012 cost the US billions of dollars in extra spending on supplies to its more than a hundred thousand personnel in Afghanistan. Eventually, Secretary of State Hillary Clinton had to apologize to Pakistan for the Salala incident in which 24 army soldiers were killed by the US military across the DL on November 26, 2011. Pakistani support is also needed as the US is getting ready for a major withdrawal from Afghanistan and the military equipment will have to be transported in the opposite direction. The alternative routes can be put to limited use; the Central Asian route is five times expensive while air lifting is 20 times more expensive.

In late 2001, the US and its NATO allies put up such a spectacular assault on Kabul that the Taliban were no match for it and they retreated without offering any resistance. Their fall was as swift as their rise to power back in 1996. A *Loya Jirga* (traditional constitutional assembly) was convened in 2002 under the leadership of Burhanuddin Rabbani, a former *Mujahideen* commander and former President of Afghanistan. Rabbani was assassinated in 2011 after he started his efforts for peace and reconciliation in Afghanistan as chief of the Afghanistan's High Peace Council. The *Jirga* also decided to hold parliamentary elections in 2003. The elections were a partial success and a former *Mujahideen* commander from Kandahar, Hamid Karzai, was elected as the President of the Islamic Republic of Afghanistan.

The Taliban were on the run after their ouster from power in late 2001. They were on the verge of elimination, when in 2003, the US and NATO allies decided to turn their attention away from Afghanistan. The Bush administration and his Neo-Conservative inner circle were too focused on ousting Saddam Hussein from power in Iraq, because he had Weapons of Mass Destruction (WMD). The WMDs were never found in Iraq after NATO toppled Saddam's regime. The Iraq invasion created more problems in Middle East than solving any. Without argument, 2012-13 has been the deadliest year since Saddam's ouster.

WHO ARE TALIBAN?

The answer depends on who do you ask this question and who is on which side of the Durand Line (DL). For a majority of Afghans, Taliban (plural; singular *Talib* which means a *madrassa* student) are simply religious students sent by ISI to destabilize their country. They believe that indigenous Taliban do not exist inside Afghanistan. The majority of people living on the Pakistani side of DL believe that the Taliban movement started in Afghan refugee camps inside Pakistan and has now spread to the entire region. It is no mystery that any Taliban killed in action on the Afghan soil are immediately claimed by the local villagers and buried with full honor (Photo 24). There is no denying the fact these Taliban fighters are close relatives of the local population where they are killed in action. The local residents in any Afghan village will tell you off the record who are various Taliban commanders and who they are related to in their village. What they say publically is a whole different story.

Analysts agree that the creation of Taliban was an indigenous Afghan process facilitated by the lawlessness of FATA. Thousands of the so-called 'Arab Afghans' and Central Asian thugs moved to FATA and adjoining Provinces in Afghanistan such as Kunar, Nuristan, Paktia, Paktika and Kandahar, all of them bordering Pakistan. However, a majority of them moved to FATA after NATO forces launched Operations Enduring Freedom and Anaconda in

2001-02. Disgusted by Pakistan's support for NATO/US allies, the 'Pakistani Taliban' launched Tehreek-e-Taliban Pakistan (TTP; Pakistan Taliban Movement) in South Waziristan Agency on December 14, 2007. The effort was led by 40 militant commanders leading approximately 40 thousand fighters (Hussain, 2013) and clandestinely supported by ISI. Subsequently, other Taliban groups and militias also emerged in North Waziristan, Kurram, Orakzai, Mohmand, and Bajaur Agencies of the FATA.

Since the Afghan war began in late 2001, the US has been bogged down in Afghanistan. Thousands of American lives have been lost and maimed and hundreds of thousands of Afghan civilians have been killed and injured. It has become the longest war in the American military history and Americans are hoping to finally close this bloody chapter at the end of 2014.

Almost 80% of Pakistan's annual budget is spent either on army (army does not allow to be audited by any civilian agency) or debt servicing while only 2% goes to education! No wonder why so many madrassas are popping up every day. These religious schools are entirely funded by Saudi and UAE money.

Photo 24: Relatives are identifying Taliban dead bodies dumped outside of an AUP station (January 2012). Some of them have been buried in the graveyard in the background.

The term "Taliban" does not specify a monolithic group of people. Taliban can be thugs, ideologues, petty criminals or in rare cases victims out there to take revenge. "The war economy that has built up over thirty years of conflict has blurred easy distinctions between farmer, opportunist, petty criminal, smuggler, narcotics dealer, mercenary, warlord, insurgent and transnational jihadist. Moreover, the contemporary insurgency is indescribable as a homogenous phenomenon and must be carefully examined in each locality it arises. Combatants fight for reasons as different as adventure and revenge, economics and honor codes. This complexity, captured in Mary Kaldor's (2007) concept of 'new wars', lends weight to the argument that the label of Taliban is something of a misnomer when applied universally to anti-government elements within Afghanistan" (Kirk, 2011).

In Pashtun culture, Taliban were religious students whose parents were poor and could not afford modern education for their children. In the old days, (before the Saudi money was showered on Pakistani madrassas) Talib (Taliban) were going from door to door to collect food for their lunch and dinner in the streets of the areas dominated by Pashtuns across the Pak-Afghan border. Today, the word Taliban is a synonym for hate. Several questions come to mind in this context; did they fail to deliver what they promised or did they try to defame Islam by their brutal punishments? There is no definitive answer to these questions, but one aspect is clear that a large number of them are unemployed people who cannot afford to put food on the table for their families. Gone are the Taliban of the past who were educated and who were considered as "religious scholars".

Taliban have lost a central command structure and now they are fighting as independent local groups. Some kind of command structure does exist but it is run by a group of opportunistic leaders. You will not find God-fearing Taliban anymore; the current Taliban are using the misguided public. Most of the original Taliban have been killed in action, and the remaining ones failed in their mission. It is believed that a large majority of the current Taliban have no clue as to what they want; they don't even know what the word *Talib* (religious student) actually mean. That's why they had no problem in destroying the Bamiyan *Buddhas* in 2001 under direct orders from *Mullah* Omar after they were declared as idols.

Taliban are not averse to modern technology, as widely believed by some analysts. They know precisely how to use modern tools to promote their ideology. In today's world, social media has become a universal tool to further ideas and Taliban are taking full advantage of this free media tool. They have opened up Facebook and Twitter accounts with extensive followings. Even a Sony PlayStation controller has been recovered from a Taliban facility, which was probably used as a detonation device. When we see Taliban propaganda videos, we often come across roomful of young men working on computers. "Once notorious for their ultra-orthodox interpretation of Islam which prescribed a complete aversion to all manifestations of modernity, the Taliban now appear to have mastered innovations in technology and put them to optimal use in their insurgency against Hamid Karzai's government and ISAF troops" (Brahimi, 2010).

The Afghan society still maintains its historic ties with brutal games. *Buzkashi* is the Afghan national game where two teams on horsebacks pull a goat towards themselves until it is fully dismembered. *Durra* (Photo 25) is another brutal game (where children hit each other with lashes until they exit a circle drawn on the dirt) which is an indicator of a primitive society. Subsequently, Taliban reintroduced lashes as a popular mode of punishment. Miscreants were nominally tried and then punished in public with lashes on their bare backs to spread terror.

"Built up by elements in Pakistani intelligence and financed with Saudi money, the Taliban waged a pitiless war on Afghan culture and traditions. At the same time they flouted the most basic human values. Stoning gay people and women who are victims of rape is barbarism pure and simple. Rather than preventing such atrocities, an Iranian-style Afghan democracy could instead confer legitimacy on those who commit them" (Gray, 2011).

The two sculptures were carved in sandstone formations in the Hazarajat region of central Afghanistan. They were built between 507 and 544 AD and were considered as the representative of classic *Gandhara* art. The Taliban drilled holes in these structures and detonated them with explosives. This event showed their real face and further exposed them to the civilized world. Some parts of these statues have now been restored.

Photo 25: Afghan teenagers are playing popular game *"Durra"* in which they hit each other with lashes (Musa Qala, April 2012).

CAN TALIBAN BE DEFEATED?

The simple answer to this question is a resounding "No", however, 'miracles' do happen. If Taliban are wiped out, it would be in the interest of everyone in the region. Taliban is a nationalist-religious movement, which wants to restore its mid-90s repressive regime with minor cosmetic changes. Taliban do not necessarily condone the international *Jihadi* movement led by Al-Qaeda. The aim of Taliban movement is to end foreign occupation of Afghanistan and once again create the Islamic Emirates of Afghanistan. Taliban across the border in Pakistan, known as Tehreek-e-Taliban Pakistan (TTP), wants the implementation of 'Shariah", a brand of Islam as defined by them. They are so determined that would love to be killed (and they call themselves 'shaheed') for this bloody 'cause'. Many analysts believe that negotiating with Taliban will strengthen their movement and not weaken it. The breakdown of Doha process in early 2013 is a testimony of that assertion. The Taliban representative blamed the US of creating a rift in the Taliban ranks and therefore announced the suspension of negotiations.

Long before the current population-centric COIN (Counter Insurgency) strategy was implemented by ISAF, it was believed that it had a low chance of success. Taliban have infiltrated every aspect of Afghan society, in fact they are part and parcel of Afghan fabric. *Mualem* Anwar is the elected member of Afghan parliament who is heavily supporting Taliban in his home Province of Helmand. As a result of his direct support, ISAF was never able

to penetrate the heavy Taliban presence in northern Helmand. The COIN strategy is focused on killing as many insurgents as possible while leaving the civilian arm of the insurgency largely intact. The latter is the true driving force behind any successful insurgency. "The Taliban are subverting and controlling the population while the Coalition is trying to find the armed Taliban, not the unarmed ones who actually subvert and infiltrate the population – chess and poker" (Danovic, 2012).

I asked a *Mullah* from Marjah, who was part of the *Shura* called by *Mullah* Omar to decide on the issue of OBL, as to why you allowed OBL to stay in Afghanistan and ready to fight the Americans but refused to hand over OBL? He told me "that there were virtually no *Shura* deliberations on this issue. I stayed at Kandahar for three days and on the final day we were told that here is the *Fatwa* , all members have signed off on it and it has been resolved that OBL will be the official guest of the Emirates of Afghanistan".

It appears as if the US and NATO allies have finally learned the lesson that the COIN strategy has not delivered the desired results and are therefore considering a faster drawdown, even earlier than the end of 2014. History is replete with examples indicating that no *Jihad* has ever ended with a negotiated settlement or through reconciliation. The Afghan tribal history shows that the stronger side is not the one to negotiate a dispute; rather it's always the weaker side who asks for reconciliation. By that yardstick, the invading forces in Afghanistan are the weaker side as they have asked the Taliban to come to a negotiating table.

Anne Stenerson of the Norwegian Foreign Institute (2010) argued that "A more realistic approach is probably to try to weaken the Taliban's coherence through negotiating with, and offering incentives to, low-level commanders and tribal leaders inside Afghanistan. The insurgent movement consists of a wide variety of actors, which may be seen as proof of its strength – but it could also constitute a weakness if properly and systematically exploited. This effort, however, requires extensive resources, both in terms of manpower and knowledge of the Afghan realities".

Coburn and Dempsey (2010) argued that civic amenities must be provided to ordinary Afghans "To counter the Taliban and achieve lasting stability in the country, it is essential to have accessible governance and justice mechanisms that allow for the peaceful, accountable, and enforceable resolution of disputes. Without such institutions, progress in security reform will not prove sustainable".

AFGHAN WAR ASYMMETRY

Despite a tech giant, the US and its NATO allies could not find a cure for the lethal IEDs (Improvised Explosive Devices). Taliban spend less than 10 USD on an IED and it can blow up an armored vehicle worth millions of dollars within seconds (Photo 26). The asymmetry does not end there. Airlifting a marine or soldier and providing proper healthcare to them end up costing the US another million or so USD.

Photo 26: War asymmetry: Graveyard of Mine-Resistant Ambush Protected (MRAP) armored vehicles destroyed by Taliban IEDs (December 2011).

Bird and Marshall (2011) argued that "despite an encouraging start, operations in Afghanistan have been restrained by under-resourcing, over-optimistic reporting, unachievable goals, and oscillating strategic incoherence". Since the US possesses a peerless fighting force, any fight with an adversary will be considered asymmetrical. According to Sims (2012), the insurgents' strategy did not require advanced weaponry. "In counter-insurgency the pro-government force loses by not winning; conversely the insurgent wins by not losing. Therefore the insurgent strategy is to demonstrate that the terrain is not secure by generating casualties buttressed by severe injuries which gain media attention, negatively influencing domestic populations".

Solving an insurgency is a complex problem and especially in a primitive society like the one in Afghanistan. Afghans have now perfected the art of playing all sides and they know exactly what to say in a given situation. "Our perspective has been clouded by the lens of Orientalism, seeking the root cause of the insurgency through a Western rather than an Afghan perspective (Malevich and Youngman, 2011). Daud Ahmadi, the Helmand Governor's spokesman, called drugs, insecurity, and corruption the three links in the chain that keep Helmand "in the dark". If the insurgency is to be defeated, all three must be addressed (Mackenzie, 2010).

In early 2008 analysts have warned that Taliban insurgency could assume dangerously high proportions (for example Dearing, 2008). The IED and suicide missions were on the rise which were aimed at three fundamental objectives; to compel the NATO to leave Afghanistan, to undermine the legitimacy of Karzai government, and to create a desperate environment for the Afghan youth so that they can easily join the Taliban mission.

THE "PAKISTAN" PROBLEM

Many analysts believe that the future of Pakistan will determine the stability of the entire South Asian region and thus has greater implications for U.S. national security. The US has been pursuing three major objectors vis-à-vis Pakistan; eliminating Al-Qaeda and the like, preventing its nuclear weapons from slipping into the wrong hands and dissuading it's military from directly ruling the country. Though the US tried to prevent further destabilization of Pakistan, recent events indicate that signs are not very promising.

A number of proposals have been under consideration to deal with the "Pakistan" problem; imposing sanctions, cutting off financial aid, drone strikes, operations by U.S. Special Forces, and declaring it as a "state sponsor of terror". At this point, no one seems to be ready to take the risk of completely isolating the nuclear-armed Muslim nation.

According to Hadley and Podesta (2012) "Washington should send clear diplomatic messages to all Pakistani political actors that military coups or other extra-constitutional ousters of a civilian government will carry drastic consequences for U.S.-Pakistani cooperation". Washington needs to shift its principal focus from military to civilian leaders and demand transparency in the utilization of military and civilian funds. It may not be feasible because of US dependence on ISI and Pakistan Army to wind down the Afghan war. Hadley and Podesta (2012) further argued that "Washington can start by lowering the public profile of the visits of its military envoys to Pakistan in favor of enhancing its interactions with civilian counterparts. Moreover, the United States should not limit its engagement with Pakistan's civilian leadership to only those serving in government but engage with all political parties and civil-society groups in the country. And Washington should cultivate relationships with the next generation of civilian leaders, who offer the best hope for a turnaround in Pakistan".

Afghans are also very concerned about the problems in the neighboring county. I asked Juma Khan who is an elder of the Shekhzai tribe in northern Helmand, "What is the problem and how do you view the solution?" His response was typical "There is absolutely no problem inside Afghanistan, once the three neighbors; Russia, Pakistan and Iran stop interfering in our country, everything will fall in place. Reconciliation and reintegration is only possible if foreign interference is eliminated. All the weapons are provided to the Taliban by our neighbors, especially Pakistan". When I asked him how do you view this interference be eliminated, his response was simple "All the weaponry is supplied by Pakistan and the international community has to exert pressure on our neighbors to stop meddling in our internal affairs". But most of the Pakistani and some international analysts disagree. They say that once the forces inside Afghanistan are united, then there will be no problem for the outside world.

A majority of Pakistanis support the notion of a Muslim *Ummah* or Muslim *Khilafah* (Nation) where all Muslims of the world will unite under one *Khalifah* (Supreme Leader). *Khilafah* has been out of scene for at least a thousand years but Pakistani Muslims have never forgotten it. Their leaders are constantly reminding them that all Muslims must be united to defeat the "evil". Who/what is this evil? There is no consensus on one definition for this evil. For the extremists, anyone who is outside their immediate circle is a *kafir* (infidel) and evil, and therefore need to be either brought inside their own circle or put to death!! For the slightly less extreme ideologues, the evil is India; they would embrace Indian music and culture, but would go to any extent to wipe out India!! For the educated Pakistanis, the evil is "The West". They can go to any extent to blame Europe and the US (and Israel) for their own failures. They can trace the origin of any problem in the world back to the West. Nobody can ask them why the West is your worst enemy; because anyone asking the question would be labeled as a traitor, and liable to be put to death.

The favorite motto for the common Pakistani and their leaders is 'blame the others'. Situation would only improve if they accepted their own fault and tried to find solution for their own problems inside Pakistan. They need to stop being misguided missiles, they need to stop worrying about Afghans, Palestinians, Kashmiris and Chechens; all of them are well capable of taking care of themselves. However, the dreams of Pan-Islamism are still alive and keeping Pakistanis distracted from their own problems.

The way Afghans are reminded by every top-level GIRoA (Government of the Islamic Republic of Afghanistan) official as to how ISI and Pakistan are responsible for all the woes in Afghanistan speaks volume for their inexperience. GIRoA has failed to grasp the gravity of the Afghan situation and the officials have been reckless in misleading their own public. At the same time these officials believe that there is nothing wrong with this country and once we defeat ISI and Pakistan, everything will get back to normal. How can you fix something which is not broken in the first place? In a country which has very little access to the outside world, the masses are bound to listen to and follow their leaders without even thinking otherwise.

"Let me ask you a question, this whole time the Americans knew where OBL was, why they invaded Afghanistan then?" asked *Molvi* Abdul Rehman, the Chief *Mullah* at Now Zad District Center mosque "Why don't the Americans invade the country where all the terrorist activity is taking place? The *Mullah* was obviously referring to its eastern neighbor, Pakistan.

Pakistan is faced with many threats to its very existence and future of the state of Jammu and Kashmir is one of them. As mentioned earlier, this problem started as soon as Pakistan came into being in 1947. The state of Jammu and Kashmir is currently divided between India and Pakistan along the Line of Control, which is not a recognized international border. Kashmiris have always indicated that they want an independent Kashmir; free of the domination of either India or Pakistan. There is a huge army presence from both India and Pakistan in Kashmir and skirmishes are not uncommon. In order to control their respective populations, both armies have committed human rights violations which are well documented by UN and human rights watchdogs.

Pakistan's entire eastern border with India is an unstable boundary and therefore Pakistan wants a peaceful and secure western border with Afghanistan. Pakistan has always tried to bring down India in Kashmir, that's why India is counteracting this pressure by making friends with Kabul. India now exerts tremendous influence in Afghanistan and it is establishing consulates along the DL. India has also started to make and win bids for the huge mineral wealth in Afghanistan.

John Gray (2011) in his cover story on perpetual warfare described the situation as follows; "Without a solution to the division of Kashmir, the Afghans will continue to be pawns in the struggle between India and Pakistan (both nuclear powers) while Iran, Russia and China watch alertly on the sidelines. Perhaps Washington could once have brokered a settlement in the region, but with President Barack Obama having declared victory 18 months in advance of a US retreat, that time is gone. A pull-out would create a geopolitical vacuum in the region. That is why – assuming a worsening economic crisis in America doesn't force the issue –US forces are unlikely to make anything like a total withdrawal any time soon".

In recent years, Pakistan has alleged that India is supporting the Pakistani Taliban as well. Christine Fair (2010) argues that "These allegations are nearly impossible to verify. For one thing, the U.S. intelligence community *does not* collect information on these activities and thus is not in a position to adjudicate empirically. Drawing upon my fieldwork in Iran (where India has a consulate in Zahidan, which abuts Pakistan's restive Baloch Province), Afghanistan, and India, anecdotal evidence suggests that, while Pakistan's most sweeping claims are ill-founded, Indian claims to complete innocence also are unlikely to be true". Rubin and Rashid (2009), writing of India's activities in Afghanistan, have argued that "pressuring or giving aid to Pakistan, without any effort to address the sources of its insecurity, cannot yield a sustainable positive outcome." Rubin and Rashid (2009) continued to propose a regional solution that suggested that the Afghanistan problem could be resolved through Kashmir.

THE POPPY CULTURE

Soon after taking power in 1996, *Mullah* Omar went back on his promise of destroying opium poppy. In 1996, the poppy cultivation was drastically down because of a ban put in place by Taliban, however, soon they found out that they need poppy. Taliban legitimized it by saying that heroin and drugs are destroying the West and therefore we should grow more poppy. Poppy cultivation shot up in the next few years and it still poses a real threat to the stability of Afghanistan. Instead of falling down, the poppy growth has mega-folded since the US invasion in 2001. Currently, about 98% of the poppy is grown in the southern and southwestern Provinces (Farah, Nimroz, Helmand, Kandahar, Zabul and Uruzgan) where Taliban are strong (see Figure 3).

Large swaths of cultivable land are covered with lush green fields of poppy, the only cash crop in the south, which bear beautiful red and white flowers in the months of March and April (Photos 28-30). The sap is collected in May, employing a large labor force, including child labor. The product is soon sent to the nearby heroin factories run by drug lords and protected by Taliban. The crop brings just a little over what the farmers will receive from growing wheat or corn, but it brings large sums of money for the drug lords. Consequently, the Taliban use force on those who refuse to grow poppy voluntarily. Almost one third of the earnings directly go to Taliban, a major source of money for funding the continued insurgency. There is an extensive drug network stretching from Pakistan, passing through Afghanistan into Iran and Central Asian Republics. The drugs then make their way into Europe and eventually reach North America. The drug network is very strong and makes every effort to make Afghanistan as unstable as possible, because instability breeds corruption, terrorism and poppy growth. The drug trafficking is an added dimension to the inter-ethnic Afghan war.

Poppy is a major source of funding for Taliban, and it cannot be fully ascertained if the international community is channeling more money or the drug networks but the source of funding is not drying up anytime soon. I asked Gulab Mengal, former Governor of Helmand, about the readiness of Afghan border forces to be strong enough to stop the heroin transport networks? "Absolutely, they can do it. The transport mafia travels in groups of two to three vehicles with not more than 10 people. They don't use large caravans or several hundred operatives. A force of 50 border police can easily take them out. The more the GIRoA spreads it's influence, the weaker the transport networks will get" Mengal said. However, Mengal didn't say whether or not they (security forces) are willing to do so.

Photo 27: Alternating fields of poppy and wheat in Kandahar (April 2012).

Photo 28: Alternating fields of poppy and wheat in Helmand (March 2012).

Photo 29: Large swaths of poppy covering fields in Helmand.

Photo 30: Hashish (Cannabis) is normally grown inside walled compounds to evade authorities (Musa Qala, 2012).

Afghanistan is an agricultural country which is heavily dependent on irrigation water. Multiple International agencies are working on dealing with water-related problems in Afghanistan and there is very little inter-agency coordination. When Civil Affair teams, USDA, IRD, NGOs and IGOs push programs on the Afghans to teach them how to grow certain crops and increase productivity, according to one USMC senior commander in Helmand, "they say; Stop it, give us water, we can grow whatever we want to. Stop giving us plants that take more water". For the outsiders, corn and cotton are the crops of choice which they want the Afghans to grow. Even to an untrained eye, these are water intensive crops and trained personnel know it well that these crops cause extensive evapo-transpiration. "This summer a lot of the cotton crop died because we ran out of water" said Lt. Col. Kustra of USMC in Helmand. There is a reason Afghans are so easily growing poppy because it is very well suited to the dry Afghan soil and it is the only cash crop available to them. One acre of poppy returns enough money to sustain one family for an entire year.

The District Governor of Now Zad (Helmand Province) Syed Murad Saadat (Photo 31) termed poppy cultivation *Haram* (against the teachings of his religion); however, he believes that the market forces outsmart the religious dictates. Despite the fact that international forces have been stationed in Afghanistan for more than ten years, large swaths of the country are still covered with poppy especially in Helmand and Kandahar. Almost the entire Afghan population is Muslim and everyone knows it well that poppy cultivation is against the teachings of Islam. Why do they still have a huge amount of poppy in Afghanistan is a perplexing question for both the locals and the outsiders.

Abdul Qayum, Deputy Governor of Now Zad District of Helmand Province (Photo 32) sees this problem as follows; "The government writ is weak in those areas where poppy is grown. Also, Taliban, under the influence from their foreign maters, are the biggest beneficiaries of poppy cultivation. *Mullah* Omar stopped poppy cultivation and termed it *haram* (against Islam) so as to improve relations with international community. Why that *fatwa* is not followed anymore? It's because the Taliban themselves are asking everyone to grow poppy". Omar himself broke this *fatwa* and asked the public to grow poppy because 'poppy (heroin) is destroying the West'. The Deputy Governor (laughingly disagreed with me) said "No, poppy is only grown in those areas where government writ is weak. I'll give you the example of Nawa as I am a resident of this District. People don't grow poppy in Nawa as they can benefit from growing licit crops. As the GIRoA is strengthened, poppy also loses traction and their transport networks are also broken. The Afghanistan border forces are there to take out these transport networks".

Photo 31: Good times: DG Murad Saadat in a good mood with an ISAF official (October 2011).

Photo 32: The author with Abdul Qayum, Deputy Governor Now Zad District (February 2012).

USDA is trying to offer alternatives, but why have we not succeeded in getting rid of this menace? Capt Raymond A. Hall, III worked as a MEF II in-bed for Agriculture and Education at Helmand PRT at Lashkar Gah where he was a direct liaison with the GIRoA officials. Prior to that, he served in Nawa and Marjah in 2009-10 as an infantry commander. He responded "Here in Helmand, they get so much more money to grow up poppy. When I first got here in 2009, the locals told me that they don't necessarily want to grow poppy but they are intimidated by the Taliban and forced to grow poppy. The Taliban would threaten our families, kidnap our children, wives and mothers and take them away if the locals would not grow poppy. Though I have seen a huge decrease in poppy being grown with the Government Led Eradication program but still a lot of poppy is being grown especially in the northern Districts of the Province. ANSF chooses to ignore the poppy fields as some of them are making money off of this and they will not push against it very hard. It is all a matter of what the country of Afghanistan chooses to do".

I was in Afghanistan during the so called 'poppy eradication campaign', I thought that that there would not be a single stalk of poppy after this campaign is over. The hype and rhetoric was so high that it raised my hopes of complete poppy eradication, however, it all proved to be a show off for the international community. The tractors brought in by international donors remained parked on the government premises and not an acre of poppy was destroyed during the entire campaign (Photo 33).

Photo 33: A long line of tractors parked at the DG's compound waiting to be deployed for poppy eradication (January 2012).

The eradication campaigns cannot be successful unless the revenue from drug trafficking is significantly brought down. Afghan poppy is the source for almost all illicit drugs in surrounding states and it is aiding to undermine stability and development in those countries. "Some studies estimate that nearly 100% of the illegal opiates reaching Afghanistan's Central Asian neighbors, as well as Turkey, Pakistan, Iran and Russia originate in poppy fields in Afghanistan, and British law enforcement officials believe that close to 90% of the heroin smuggled into the country is derived from Afghan sources" (Blanchard, 2007).

Maass (2011) believes that Afghanistan has achieved a virtual monopoly in the drug business. "With a current share of 93 per cent of the global market in illicit opiates (opium, morphine and heroin), Afghanistan has achieved a monopoly. Recently Afghanistan has also become one of the world's leading suppliers of cannabis (hashish)". There is no easy solution to Afghan drug epidemic. "Linking the Afghan mission with the nonsensical 'war on drugs' has been predictably counterproductive. Destroying drug production – the Americans at one point thinking of spraying the whole of Helmand Valley with weed killer to wipe out the opium fields –would also have destroyed much of the Afghan economy" (Gray, 2011).

There must be a coordinated effort to limit demand for various opiates. A re-shaped military and intelligence strategy must be combined with intensive diplomacy, along with reforms in police, judicial, and economic sectors will lead to a multi-pronged approach to tackle the drug menace. "Targeted development programs will lead to more employment opportunities and less dependence on drug trafficking. As the biggest donor with the largest number of deployed troops there, the United States should take the lead in revitalizing the international community's strategy toward Afghanistan (Peters, 2009)".

With US/NATO pullout in works, poppy cultivation has increased by 50% in 2013 from the previous year, according to a UN report published in November, 2013. Currently, 516,000 acres of poppy is being grown in Afghanistan and hence maintaining its spot as the World's No. 1 poppy producer. Similarly, opium production rose by 11% from 3,700 tons to more than 5,500 tons in the same time period. These figures are by no means an encouraging sign of the direction in which the insurgency is headed.

Chapter 12
THE AFGHAN GOVERNMENT

Afghanistan is divided into 34 provinces and each province is further divided into varying number of districts which are roughly equivalent to the size of a US county. District administration is headed by a District Governor (DG) locally called *Olaswal* which translates to 'public administrator'. The district administration consists of various directorates or *'Mudiriats'* such as education, irrigation, agriculture, transport, water, public health etc. Their job description is not always clearly defined and sometimes one department falls under two or more provincial directors. As an example, water falls under HAVA, DAIL and MoM. Similarly, it is not clear as to who the directors are answerable to? It is not clearly defined if they report to the DG or provincial ministers. There is virtually no communication between the district level directors and their provincial counterparts.

Afghans have managed with minimal governmental presence and therefore the Afghan President has sometimes been dubbed as the 'Mayor of Kabul'. Outside of Kabul, the president had little influence as DG, DCOP, local *Jirga*s and tribal elders wielded more powers. Lately, two national elections have been held and two houses of parliament, lower house (National Assembly; *Wolasi Jirga*) and upper house (Senate; *Masharano Jirga*) have been established. In Provinces, the Governors have been assigned very few duties from the central government and remained largely as symbolic figures. The real powers rested with the head of the tribe and *Jirga* (a group of influential elders in every tribe).

AFGHAN NATIONAL SECURITY FORCES
(ANSF)

ANSF is divided into Afghan National Army (ANA) and Afghan National Police (ANP). There is virtually no Air Force in the country, though international efforts have been re-doubled in the past few years to create a sizeable air power for the landlocked country. Police is the most diverse force and is further divided into;

1. Afghan Uniformed Police (AUP)
2. Afghan National Civil Order Police (ANCOP)
3. Afghan Border Police (ABP)
4. Afghan Local Police (ALP) and
5. Counter Narcotics Police of Afghanistan (CNPA)

Specialized units such as CID (Criminal Investigation Division) and CTP (Counter Terrorism Police) are smaller organizations within ANP. AUP constitute the bulk of police personnel and has traditionally remained a protocol force dealing very little with maintaining law and order. ANA has been dismembered and recreated several times since the Afghan coups began in 1973. It is not a professional organization rather it serves its respective ethnic leaderships.

When I asked Capt Hall about the combat readiness of ANSF, he was not very hopeful "In some respects, the ANSF is ready to take over; we have trained them well enough but they still expect us to get things done for them, knowing that we have more assets, resources, capabilities and finances. So I think right now they are leaning on us and trying to get as much out of us as they can. In other areas such as education with lot of schools that we have built, they are still seeking teachers and monetary support for that. Nationwide, there is a 51% national deficit rate for teachers. So there are areas in which they are doing well and then in others they are very short".

US President Barak Obama (May 2012), while addressing his troops at the Bagram Air Base, described the situation as, "But over the last three years, the tide has turned. We broke the Taliban's momentum. We've built strong Afghan security forces. We devastated al Qaeda's leadership, taking out over 20 of their top 30 leaders. And one year ago, from a base here in Afghanistan, our troops launched the operation that killed OBL. The goal that I set—to defeat al Qaeda and deny it a chance to rebuild—is now within our reach".

Lately, there has been a lot of emphasis on formation of ALP. The basic tenant for hiring ALP is flawed from the very start, however, it is a good means of bribing the local elders into supporting GIRoA and the CF. General Stavridis (2011) explains the process of hiring for ALP as "Someone has to hire the local young males in an attempt to diminish their desire to assist the insurgency, effectively draining the manpower pool available to the insurgents. If these men have a job, they are less likely to be bored and they will not tend to be as bitter toward security forces that might be perceived as occupiers. This also provides a manpower pool that may be used to provide local security and inject money into the local economy. When this occurs, local markets will reopen and prosperity will begin to return (Photo 34). If security forces or other government entities do not hire the local youths, they will likely take up arms for ideological reasons, for economic purposes, or out of boredom". As the premise of the hiring process is false the rest explained by General Stavridis is also not true "Once this stage is reached, operations shift from clearing to holding and building. In these phases, a government must be formed if one is not present, and the government must then provide the services that the people expect".

Gray (2011) summed the failure of ANSF "…. where government is weak and lacking in legitimacy, and where allegiance to any authority has long been a tradable commodity, it should be obvious that improving the training of local forces will not ensure their loyalty". Drugs (Photo 35), desertions and corruption are the three corners of the failure of ANSF. Ethnic factionalism is one reason several groups have warned as early as May 2010, that the Afghan National Army is 'incapable of fighting the insurgency on its own, the other reasons being drug addiction, illiteracy, and desertion" (Baldauf, 2012). Police chiefs have been involved in supplying ammunition to Taliban; DCOP Attaullah in Helmand Province was reportedly involved in providing arms and ammunition to Taliban. A general lack of interest in their duties has been noticed in the Afghan security forces (Photo 36).

Photo 34: ISAF officials contributing to the local economy (January 2012).

Photo 35: An off –duty policeman is smoking hashish with little children around right in front of his police station (Now Zad, 2012).

Afghan security forces are not equipped to deal with the threat from the Haqqani Network in their current state. There are real threats to a stable Afghanistan and the Haqqani Network operating from Pakistan is just one of them. This terrorist organization is a threat to regional stability as well as it hosts international terrorists with objectives in Central Asia, India, and the Gulf States. ANSF lacks the intelligence, and sophisticated command and control mechanisms required to reclaim the enemy support zones in the southern half of the country. "The United States must not abruptly shift the mission of its forces in Afghanistan from counter-insurgency to security force assistance. U.S. forces cannot curtail or cease offensive operations in the areas South of Kabul in Regional Command East in 2012. The United States and its Afghan partners must dismantle the Haqqani Network's strongholds in Khost, Paktika, and Paktia and contain the organization's expansion toward Kabul prior to a shift in mission. Failure to do so will present a strategic threat to U.S. national security interests in Afghanistan" (Dressler, 2012).

Capt Michael C. Petit (USMC), who served as the Civil Affairs Team Leader in northern Helmand, was more forthcoming about the role of CF in this regard "We focus too much on fighting the insurgency – engaging them in actual combat – and not enough on the non-kinetic aspect of the conflict such as government capacity building, peace and reintegration programs, and professionalizing the indigenous security forces. The key to long-term stability is not the military defeat of the insurgency, it is the emergence of a popular, self-sustaining government that provides the population with an alternative to the Taliban".

Photo 36: An ANP cop has hanged his AK-47 by the barbed (concertina) wire while guarding a DG's compound in northern Helmand (March 2012).

The Afghan society is tolerant of older men keeping *'chai boys'* for their sexual pleasures and ANSF also suffers from this menace. In 2012, there were nine chai boys for the DCOP of Marjah District in central Helmand Province while the DCOP for Now Zad content himself with only two. Ironically, Afghans claim to be the best Muslims in the world. To ordinary Afghans, the rest of the world is suffering from immorality and going in the wrong direction. Animals, especially goats, are occasionally used for performing sexual acts. Taliban have effectively used it as a diversion to avoid the ISAF surveillance instruments. The young, inexperienced Marines and soldiers would be busy startling over these acts while Taliban would be busy emplacing IEDs at a nearby location.

According to Goodson and Johnson (2011), the US has spent roughly 18 billion USD since 2002 on the ANA. It is difficult to get accurate numbers on the actual size of ANA soldiers present for duty. DoD refers to ANA troop strength as 'trained and equipped' which is a vague phrase for reporting ANA numbers in press releases. This number does not equate to the number of ANA troops present for duty. I spoke to several ANA soldiers and they said they are only present for duty for about 6 months in any given year. It is estimated that one third of the ANA is now disappearing every year through desertions (18 percent) and non-reenlistment (60 percent). "Interestingly, the Army's Center for Army Lessons Learned (CALL) in Fort Leavenworth, Kansas, had a statistician analyze ANA growth and attrition rates in 2005 and concluded that the ANA could never grow larger than 100,000 men, because at that point the annual attrition losses would equal the maximum number of new recruits entering the force each year" (Goodson and Johnson, 2011).

It will simply not be possible for the Afghan government to maintain such a large force. "With the Afghan government's total annual revenue hovering around 4 billion USD and the Obama administration's budget request for fiscal year 2012 of 12.8 billion USD to train and equip Afghanistan's expanding army and national police force, it will be extremely difficult for Afghanistan to manage and sustain a force of that size and expense over the long term without protracted external financial and material support" (Goodson and Johnson, 2011).

It appears as if the international community has created another monster in the form of ANSF. In the best possible scenario, ANA will break up along ethnic lines and will join their respective warlords once NATO leaves in 2014. GySgt Timothy A. Noller of USMC characterized the readiness of the ANSF as follows; "It depends on numbers and their ability to replenish themselves". There are reports that increasing number of Taliban are being recruited in ANSF and whenever they get a chance, they turn against their own fellow soldiers and policemen while at the same time carrying out the so called "green on blue" attacks (insider attacks where ANSF attacks ISAF). It seems like the will to fight the "Taliban" has evaporated with time. "The Afghan soldiers will fight if American advisors are alongside them; the Afghans will crumble without them" (West, 2011). A national army cannot withstand the pressures of 21st century if it is entirely dependent on an outside force.

AFGHAN CORRUPTION

Money and corruption go hand in hand and Afghan people have witnessed unprecedented levels of corruption since the US invasion of 2001. The Afghans are as worried about corrupt practices as the international donor agencies. In a country, where institutions are weak and individuals are strong, misappropriation of funds can become a normal business practice. The international community has spent billions of dollars on developmental projects, but one can't see its effects on the ground; where did that money go? I asked a top government official in Kabul. "By God I was not here when that money was spent and I don't see it either, this question should be asked from the donors as to where you have buried that money! [Laughing]. Developmental projects of high visibility should have been initiated but we only see sporadic development" he responded.

Four billion USD leave Afghanistan annually, it is partly contributed by our tax payers money and partly from the drug trafficking. The money is routed to financial institutions in Dubai and other Gulf states. The entire salaries of the government officials are paid from our tax payer's money. Even the gas in all government vehicles is given from the gas pool for NATO. Most of it is sold in the local market. A school repair in northern Helmand cost the US tax payers around 400,000 USD, the actually money spent on the project was less than 18,000 USD (Photos 37-40).

Photo 37: Governor Gulab Mengal of Helmand Province inaugurating a newly renovated high school for boys (August 2011).

Photo 38: Afghan children are sitting on the floor in a high school.

Photo 39: FET members distributing supplies to mark the inauguration of a school repaired with US money.

Photo 40: Two FET members and a member of USAID at the inauguration of the school in northern Helmand.

Capt. Hall described the state of Afghan corruption as follows; "I received all kinds of complains about corrupt officials and contractors. An Afghan engineer stopped a major project and asked the contractor for 50,000 Afghanis if he wants to continue working on the project. As a United States Marine, I don't get involved with that stuff, I stay out of things of that nature, but at the same I have seen many times corrupt dealings on the side".

An Afghan official I spoke to blamed the international community for the misuse of funds and lack of transparency. Citing the USMC teams in Now Zad District of Helmand, he said "The previous Marine teams did not negotiate the contracts and excluded the District government from the process. This led to corruption in all directions. The present team has started to include the GIRoA in decision making and you can see that we have achieved much better results. GIRoA and international community want to eliminate Al-Qaeda from this country. If funds are misappropriated, they end up in wrong hands and it strengthens Al-Qaeda which is good for neither GIRoA nor the international community. There is a strong need for both parties to pay more attention to this issue. I believe more blame goes to GIRoA in this regard. In my view the major problem is that corrupt officials are rarely removed from their positions in this country".

Rep. John F. Tierney, Chair Subcommittee on National Security and Foreign Affairs Committee on Oversight and Government Reform of the U.S. House of Representatives, explained in June 2010 the way our tax dollars end up in the hands of Taliban, ".....the Department of Defense designed a contract that put responsibility for the security of vital U.S. supplies on contractors and their unaccountable security providers. This arrangement has fueled a vast protection racket run by a shadowy network of warlords, strongmen, commanders, corrupt Afghan officials, and perhaps others. Not only does the system run afoul of the Department's own rules and regulations mandated by Congress, it also appears to risk undermining the U.S. strategy for achieving its goals in Afghanistan".

The same sentiments have been echoed by other analysts as well. "It is time that we as Americans – in government, in the media, and as analysts and academics – took a hard look at the causes of corruption in Afghanistan. The fact is that we are at least as much to blame for what has happened as the Afghans, and we have been grindingly slow to either admit our efforts or correct them" (Cordesman, 2010).

GIRoA AND REINTEGRATION

The Afghans have always preferred to live in a tribal society and repulsed any foreign invaders and influences. They had their own tribal policing and disputes were resolved in a traditional setting. For centuries, Afghans have had a parallel system of conflict resolution called the *Jirga* System and people have turned to this traditional system instead of bringing their disputes to the DG's compound. When the US decided to switch to "Nation Building" in Afghanistan, they chose to revamp the government system in the country and installed District governments and a top-heavy bureaucracy. Most Districts were given up to 35 officials including two prosecutors, a *Huquq* judge (to resolve civil disputes) and a District judge. In most cases they could not attract any case and were simply paid by the US taxpayers' money. I asked a GIRoA official about this situation and his response was "Personnel are essential. Slowly and gradually they will start receiving cases. General public is not aware of the presence of these officials. Also, very little area of the District is under GIRoA control. Once the GIRoA writ is expanded to the entire District, then all these officials will start getting cases. Since the arrival of these officials three months back, I have not received a single case which fell under their purview. And it's a good thing that so far no cases have been brought before us! [Laughing]". While working with both District and provincials level GIRoA officials I noted that there was virtually no connection between the District level directors and their provincial level ministers.

In most cases, the new form of government failed to deliver for a number of reasons and often led to a mockery of the system by the locals. Traditionally, the Afghan District level government always consisted of only two officials; an *Olaswal* (District Administrator) and a *Komandan* (District Police Chief). When a heavy bureaucracy was imposed on all the Districts, it was an alien form of government and predictably, it created more problems and contributed very little to the overall development and stabilization of the country. One of the major issue which was created by this form of government was rampant corruption as the salary of government officials was not enough for their lavish lifestyles. When an administrator is called a "Governor", he entitles himself/herself to perks and privileges!

The way we have created a "Society of Entitlement" in Afghanistan will have its repercussions in the near future. At home we are always complaining that why we have people on welfare and in Afghanistan we are running the biggest welfare society in American history. An entire generation of Afghans is growing up in such an environment and even the Afghan children are now a part of it. You will always see little kids asking for candy whenever they see a '*Khariji*, a term loosely defining foreigners. Free wheat, free vegetable seeds, free fertilizers, you name it and it is given free of cost to the farmers. Interestingly enough, a majority of these freebies end up in the local market! There is not enough land to grow all these licit crops as the land is taken by the golden leaf of poppy.

The tribal structure dictates that personalities have to be respected and they have to be disproportionately stronger than their followers. As an example, when Taliban took out Commander Koka from Musa Qala District in Helmand, it weakened the ANSF defenses and led to subsequent attacks by Taliban on the District center. His brother was picked as the next DCOP, but he also fell to Taliban a year later and that was a serious blow to GIRoA in northern Helmand. Tribal structure also demands being suspicious and alert; President Karzai's personal bodyguards are not Afghans; a reflection on how everyone is distrustful of everyone else.

GIRoA suffers from an acute shortage of qualified manpower. Most of the current government officials are very young and lack the necessary experience to run a government successfully. Brain drain in recent decades has affected all south Asian nations, but Afghanistan is really hard hit by this menace. The highly qualified doctors, engineers, teachers and military personnel have moved to Europe and North America. A large number of qualified personnel are fighting alongside the Taliban and it is an uphill task to bring them to the fold of GIRoA. "How these misguided people will rejoin the government; keeping in view the fact that the ARRP (Afghan Reintegration and Reconciliation Program) has not produced much results so far" I asked the District Governor of Zaranj in Nimroz Province. He explained it as follows;

"There are ARRPs at the District, provincial, national and international levels. There are two aspects of the ARRP; the internal one is designed to bring individuals to the government fold and the external one is intended for larger peace. You can see that the external ARRP has started functioning in Qatar and it is taking the peace process forward. In terms of the internal peace process, individuals have no choice but to come to terms with the Afghanistan government". He further went on "You can see that the GIRoA is getting stronger day by day; AUP and ANA are increasing in number and powers are being transferred to the GIRoA on a gradual basis. Once the GIRoA transition is complete, then these people (Taliban) have absolutely no excuse to fight; GIRoA is an Islamic system consisting of former Mujahedeen fighters. Jihad is over, a Muslim cannot fight another Muslim, so they (Taliban) will have to sit down and reintegrate. In my opinion, low level Taliban commanders are clever; they have seen the writing on the wall. They are thinking that if *Mullah* Omar and others will be offered big positions in the government, they should also vie for some type of position".

Chapter 13
DEVELOPMENT

ASYMMETRIC DEVELOPMENT
North vs. South

There is a major north-south division in the country; separating Pashtuns in the south and east extending across the DL from Tajiks, Uzbeks and Turkmen in the north and northwest. However, all ethnicities are mixed to a certain degree and pockets of Pashtuns can be found in the north and vice versa. The Ghazni-Herat line is generally considered as the boundary between north and south, though by no means this is a precise boundary (Figure 14). A comparable situation would be northeastern vs. southern United States. Kabul, Ghazni, Herat and Farah are still offering amenities to its millions of residents, however, Kandahar, Lashkar Gah and smaller urban centers in the south are in shambles. An entire generation grew up in a perpetual war and very few knew how a stable Afghanistan looked like. Kabul resembled any modern city and night clubs and dance clubs were a way of life in Afghanistan until 1973.

There are very few cities in the entire country (Figure 14); Kabul, Ghazni, Kandahar, Mazar-i-Sharif and Herat being the only major urban centers with only 10% of the entire population living there. The rest of the population lives in villages which are almost entirely made up of mud walls (Photo 41). One ethnic group, called the *Kochis*, are nomads and live their entire life in temporary housings or tents. People living in urban centers are far more educated and civilized than the rural population. There are virtually no civic facilities available in the rural areas and whatever little was available has been destroyed by four decades of mismanagement, war and mayhem.

Photo 41: Afghan nomad (*kochi*) girls standing in their dilapidated abodes in Khan Nashin (Photo by R. Khattak, April 2011).

A north-south divide is also a significant boundary in terms of conservative vs. liberal values. The south in general is more conservative (Taliban originated in and are strongly supported by the south). Wahabi Islam (Saudi brand Islam) is on the rise and getting momentum mainly in the south. The north is more liberal and just before the Soviet invasion Kabul was full of life like any other European city. Some sections of the population in Kabul, Herat and Mazar-i-Sharif have remained liberal even before the US invasion. Under their robes, *burqas* and *chadaris*, they wear designer jeans and t-shirts and only show them when no religious fanatics are around. They attend secret concerts and cinemas. They watch Hindi soap operas and Bollywood movies and dream of a day when they will be free to choose their own lives.

The few industries present in the country are concentrated in the north, mostly around Kabul. Industrial development is almost non-existent in the south. Traditionally, high seats of learning were concentrated in Ghazni, Kabul, Jalalabad, Herat and Mazar-i-Sharif and this trend still continues. The literacy rate is much higher in the north as compared to the south. Some of this can be explained by the huge income disparities between the poor and the rich. According to the CIA World Fact Book, the average Afghani makes less than 1000 USD per year and 38% of the economy depends on subsistence farming. The unemployment rate is as high as 40% and the number of people living below the poverty line is 53%. In a country where the median age is 17.6 years and life expectancy is only 44, a huge generation gap is inevitable.

Shia-Sunni division has always led to massacres of the minority Shia Hazaras. They are strongly supported by Iran and is the main reason why Iran is involved in Afghanistan. Pashto-Dari divide is often sharp and may not always involve the Pashtuns. This division is so intense that the President has to make his speech in both languages in order to make it acceptable to a wider audience. Even the president's attire also represents this subdivision.

There has always been a trust deficit between the two halves, mainly because Afghanistan has traditionally been reined by rulers from the south (especially from Kandahar). One would imagine that these rulers would give more attention to the south simply because they hailed from there but that is not the case. Unfortunately, once these rulers reached Kabul, they concentrated all their energies on the north and as a result the south remained neglected. The pro-Kabul nature of the northern population may have contributed to this trend among the Afghan rulers. The net result is that the north has still some semblance of civility even after four decades of destruction. Subsequently, the south has gone from bad to worse and created a safe haven for terrorists and religious fundamentalists. . For this simple reason, I have placed more emphasis on the south throughout this book. The north has escaped relatively unscathed from the brutality of successive invasions and civil wars and hence the infrastructure is in a relatively better shape as compared to the south

The north-south division has, at times, led to heightened tension and speculation that this country should be divided into two parts; one mainly for Pashtuns and one for the rest of the ethnicities. As a recent example, Sudan has been divided along a north-south line in 2011.

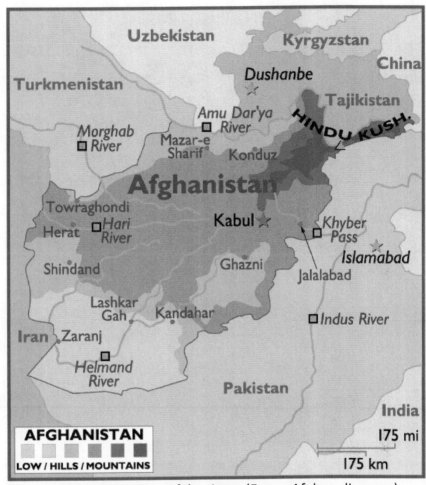

Figure 14: Major cities in Afghanistan (From: Afghan diaspora).

WOMEN DEVELOPMENT

Afghan women have suffered many setbacks in the past four decades. They have been restricted to their homes, sexually and physically abused, and barred from society in general. Afghan women played a vital role in everyday life in 1950s and 60s but the war has brought nothing but misery for them. The Taliban rule of 1996-2001 was especially a hard time period for Afghan women. They were completely banned from public life and little girls were subjected to harsh physical abuse. Girl schools were closed and women were ordered not to go out in public without a male relative (*Mahram*).

Traditionally, women had played minimal role in the male-centric Afghan society. Rural women had remained at a particular disadvantage as they had to be completely covered from head to toe in traditional gowns called *burkas/chadaris* (Photo 42). On the contrary, women in the few urban centers have been able to break loose the shackles and modestly contribute to the society.

It appears that the middle class women have entirely disappeared from the Afghan society. We either see women on the extreme left, very liberal and detached from the mainstream Afghan society, or we see far right, burka-clad women, who are also detached from everyday life on the Afghan streets. Social ills have kept this gulf as wide as possible. The religious and social structures do not allow Afghan women to play an active role in all spheres of life. It is a common practice to pay the father of the bride a handful of money at the time of marriage (a form of dowry); the current going price is about 9000 USD. This is a large amount of money by any stretch of imagination and therefore illegal means have to be used to acquire such wealth. The birth rate is 2.63%, infant mortality is 15% and the average woman has 6.58 children. The infant mortality is higher for female babies indicating that some female babies maybe killed in favor of males.

Photo 42: Afghan women clad in *burkas/chadaris* (Photo by R. Khattak, May 2011).

Social programs by various non-government entities have not put a big dent on the plight of Afghan women. UN has launched various programs to address the reproductive health issues with not much success. International NGOs were largely discouraged by Taliban and some were expelled who were specifically focused on women issues. There is no reliable data on women health but the short life span of 44 years tells the story (Photo 43). Religious beliefs make it very difficult to implement any initiatives; Islam does not allow any contraceptives. Lack of healthcare facilities and the tribalized structure of the Afghan society make it very harsh on children to receive timely treatment (Photos 44-48). US and NATO allies have initiated a large number of projects to alleviate women plight in Afghanistan, but the results varied greatly; only a few met with success. "How well received the women's projects were in your area and how they complemented the battle space?" I asked members of the Female Engagement Team (FET) working in Now Zad District of northern Helmand.

"In short term the Women Center (Photo 49) is a success but in long term I doubt that it will have any success. Once the Coalition Forces (CF) leave, the Center will pretty much disappear" said Sgt Comfort. The local ANA and AUP soldiers were more apprehensive of the presence of a women center and Sgt Benham, Incharge of FET, urged the DG to save the Women Center from ANA and AUP threats.

Another example of a failed imagination is funding projects where they don't belong. A micro loan of 5000 USD was extended to a family in northern Helmand to open a "Women's Beauty Parlor" (Photo 50). The family was smart enough and purchased a few cosmetic items worth about 100 USD and sent the rest of the money to Kabul where they were permanently residing. "I probably would not have spent this money on this project" said Sgt Comfort. She continued "more women entrepreneurs should have been funded so that a large section of the community would benefit". FET recommended that the beauty parlor should be shifted to the women's center, but the husband of the parlor owner interfered and did not let it happen. I asked Sgt Benham about the present and future of women in Afghanistan; "I wish I can say that women in Afghanistan have a positive future" she responded.

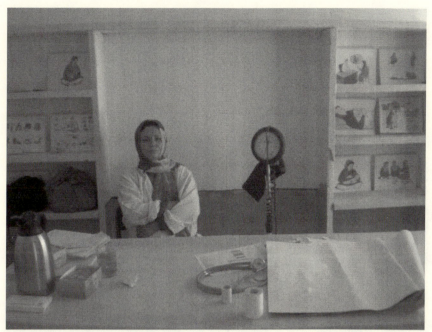

Photo 43: Located in Helmand, an Afghan doctor is sitting in her clinic with scant facilities. The blood pressure monitor is not in working condition since its arrival (November 2011).

Photo 44: A US Marine is showing the use of dental hygiene to Afghan kids in Helmand (November, 2011).

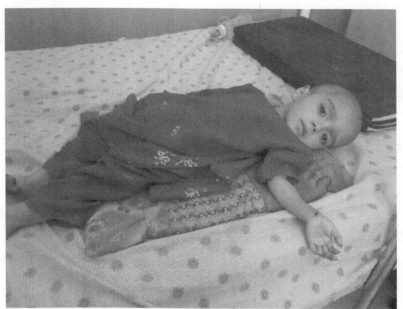

Photo 45: A little girl suffering from an undiagnosed blood disorder is lying on a bed in her hometown of Khan Nashin because of lack of healthcare facilities (Photo by R. Khattak, June 2011).

Photo 46: A little girl sitting in unhygienic conditions in her home of Khan Nashin (Photo by R. Khattak, July 2011).

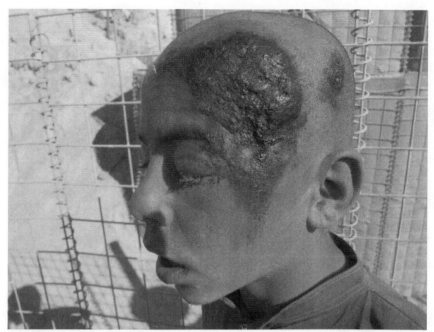

Photo 47: Home medicine is applied to a serious skin disease in a young boy (Photo by R. Khattak, August 2011).

Photo 48: Afghan kids are happy with dental hygiene products they received from the US Marine. (Photo by R. Khattak).

Photo 49: Women Center in northern Helmand (December 2011).

Photo 50: A view of the 5000 USD beauty parlor in Now Zad District Center (November 2011).

I spoke to Deputy DG (Now Zad) about the projects initiated by the Marines in his District. "There are a couple of Marine-funded projects which don't make any sense to me such as the women beauty parlor and motor cycle repair facility. The beauty parlor has not received a single customer so far and I don't believe that Now Zadian women would even be willing to go there". These and other projects clearly indicate the unfamiliarity of the US/NATO civil and military decision makers with the Afghan culture. "The beauty parlor is a completely senseless project. Sometimes we are doubted that maybe the government was involved in this scam, but nobody consulted us when awarding this project. If I was consulted, I would have spent this money on repairing 20 shops which would have an obvious benefit and high visibility. I would have spent this money on building a new school! So I totally agree with you that this project doesn't make any sense. So this money was a complete wastage of resources. People in Now Zad were doubting us anyways but now they have raised eyebrows over the integrity of the Marines as well. In the one year I have been in this District, I have not even heard about this project, let alone it's utility. On the other hand when we demand money for our office supplies and computers, which are essential to our survival, we are shown the door [Laughing]" he further said.

When I asked Sgt Benham about the Afghan culture, her response was interesting "It absolutely astonishes me as to how people can be killed for absolutely nothing. A brother can kill his brother; it's very painful to me".

RECONSTRUCTION AND DEVELOPMENT

"Afghans really like milk, somebody dropped an American cow in our backyard, and we will get as much milk from it as possible". Abdul Mutalib, District Governor Marjah (Helmand Province).

Afghanistan has never been popular for sky rise buildings or other spectacular structures. However, it has remained a center of culture and arts and crafts for centuries. In terms of infrastructure, there were virtually no major road networks in Afghanistan; the only national highway was a four-lane circular road connecting major cities with the capital Kabul. The four decades of unabated warfare has put tremendous pressure on the crumbling infrastructure in the country. The Taliban inflicted a severe blow to the historic and cultural heritage and they intentionally targeted schools to keep the country in dark. The country is in dire need of roads, schools, hospitals and major civilian infrastructures. When the entire country is dependent on foreign aid; one must prioritize as to how that money will be spent.

The US decided to rebuild the entire country especially after the British bombed the southern Provinces during 2007-08. Huge sums of money were allocated for various projects and low-level commanders were given emergency funds (Commanders' Emergency Response Program; CERP) to award projects up to 5000 USD. "Four years ago Afghanistan was the 'Wild Wild West' of America while right now we are focusing on governance and economic lines of operation, developing the infrastructure, working with GIRoA and the Regional Command, SouthWest" said Capt. Hall who served in Helmand in 2011-12. "The U.S. has spent 22.34 billion USD on governance and development in Afghanistan since it invaded the country following the September 11 attacks, much of that on projects to build roads, schools, power plants and irrigation systems. In the past two years alone, 800 million USD was earmarked for infrastructure projects" (Vogt, 2013).

Close to a trillion USD have now been spent on the Afghan war, of course most of this money was spent on kinetics and tactics rather than reconstruction and development. A number of very large permanent military bases have been built around the country including Bagram Air Base, Camp Leatherneck, Camp Dwyer, and Shindand Air Base. All these bases have ostentatious dining facilities and fast food restaurants. When I asked L.Cpl. Tom Poggyseisma about how he viewed Camp Leatherneck, He said "Leatherneck is hugely developed and I was expecting it to be a more austere environment" So even for soldiers and marines, these major camps are a bit too much.

"We are building schools with outrageous amounts of money, a lot of them aren't even open right now, or became AUP or ALP posts. Some of these schools were converted into Elders' *Shura* Halls" said Lt. Col. Kustra, who served with Marine Expeditionary Force (MEF) II in Helmand.

It appears like most of the structures built by ISAF will be converted into personal property once the Coalition Forces leave in 2014. Most commanders I spoke to believe that we have created a false economy, addiction and expectations which the Afghans and GIRoA will never be able to maintain. "We have set them up for failure" said one senior US Army Commander. "We spent over 100 million dollars in Marjah in the past year alone. Probably, over half of this money went to peoples' pockets and now they are asking where is this money?" said one CAG leader. There was no coordination among various agencies responsible for developmental activities at the District and provincial levels. Multiple agencies such as SRAD, British Engineers, USMC, DST, State Department, C-9 and G-9, were crowded in one District making decisions on funding. In most cases, the local BSO did not even know the presence of, for example, if someone is visiting from the State Department.

In central Helmand, the elders asked for 30,000 USD to clean one block of a canal, which the locals have always cleaned on their own before the US involvement in Afghanistan. "They (the Afghans) don't really care what the project is for. They want the money from the project that they can cut out of it" he further said. You cannot see these huge amounts of money on the ground. GIRoA can build a bridge or two in any given year but the Afghans will never be happy with that. In northern Helmand, the elders and GIRoA officials used the road closure an excuse to utilize the resources much needed for ISAF. All the GIRoA officials were airlifted to and from Lashkar Gah. The DG was given a VIP chopper whenever he wanted to travel outside of his District. Even the local teachers were airlifted every 2-3 months when they would visit their home towns. It all ended up costing the US millions of dollars. In late 2012, when ISAF refused to airlift teachers back to their District, they organized a huge protest by brining all the students of the District center and staged a sit-in at the entrance of FOB Now Zad (Photo 51). All these examples lead us to believe that Money As A Weapon System (MAAWS) is not an effective policy. "Although CERP was effective at capitalizing on security gains through a short-term purchase of loyalty or information, its use for non-security and nonemergency purposes has been highly criticized" (Patterson and Robinson, 2011).

Photo 51: High school teachers organized a student sit-in at the entrance of FOB Now Zad (March 2012) to demand airlifting of their teachers.

The US involvement has created a culture of entitlements and a welfare state because the "Americans like to throw money at problems". It is ironic that those who vehemently oppose a welfare state within the United States are in favor of running one in Afghanistan. The US military has been using money to achieve its objectives in Afghanistan since the war began in 2001. Money As A Weapon System – Afghanistan (MAAWS-A) is an official policy with online and offline resources available to the commanders. Capt. Hall expressed reservations about the use of money as a weapon system "In some respects we have actually set the Afghans up for failure because we have built so many things for them and we have poured time, money and effort into projects and initiatives and get things started for them. Afghanistan truly cannot uphold these things once we leave. The question is can they continue to build the capacity, can they have the funds to continue on with budgeting and conducting operational maintenance? And if they can't, then all of this that we have poured in will go to waste. Things are going to break down because they can't keep up with them. The Afghans have to make a choice whether to pay the internet and power bills and buy farm equipment and crop seeds or replace brand new trucks for every officer in the government sector as we have just entitled them to".

In one case in Kandahar, the DG was not willing to inaugurate a school which was refurbished with 150,000 USD. The contractor put new windows and covered the mud walls with a cement layer. It was such a terrible job that the DG refused to take any credit for it and made a lot of complaints. It was a complete waste of money. The USAID insisted that it was a success as the school was repaired through the Afghan process. It was the idea of them working through the system, but the USAID professionals never realized that it was American tax payers' money! "Building schools and hospitals may be a fine thing, but it will count for nothing when teachers and doctors are terrorized and killed after allied forces make their inevitable withdrawal from much of the country" (Gray, 2011).

A senior High school teacher, who was sitting in Lashkar Gah along with his 20 colleagues to be airlifted to their school in Now Zad, called me 89 times in less than 2 hours because his flight got cancelled due to bad air and he wanted to know why his flight got cancelled!

One senior military Commander characterized this situation as follows: "We don't have unlimited money so we have got to use it wisely with the least negative effects for GIRoA. When I tried to put some sense into all this, I was accused of plotting an 'insurgency' against them. We should have done a better job of spending tax payers' money. Now that we are transitioning to GIRoA and the little money we are spending is also spent through them, but they are still keep coming back to us as they are not willing to make hard decisions. They are smart; the Afghans played us very well, it is our fault, not theirs. They are very good at manipulating us. Most Americans don't realize how smart they are. We under-estimate them [the Afghans] all the time in their ability to play that game. The Afghans have realized that the money will run out soon so now I have noticed a very greedy and predatory behavior". Over the years, the Afghans have perfected the art of saying the right thing to the right person. They will only say stuff which you want to hear. The Afghans want to milk this cow to the last drop".

"We came up with bright ideas but the Afghans accepted those which had money for their own pockets, no one cared about the collective good of their own country" said one senior commander. "However, there was no dearth of foolish ideas; for a country with one of the lowest literacy rates in the world, we are building internet cafes" he further said. He went on to say, "The micro-grants were a terrible idea, where in the world you have seen money being given away without an ownership in it? We don't have a clue what the Afghans want or are capable of". As an example, USAID/DOS require that contracts should be awarded to those who have a dossier to prove that they have been successful contractors! Hazrat, Rozi, and Asmat were three contractors who worked in northern Helmand and never had a dossier to present to DST. As a result, contracts were awarded to influential contractors who simply pocketed the money instead of spending it on developmental projects.

It appears like we have created a white elephant and the moment CF leave Afghanistan and there is an enhanced donor fatigue, this entire infrastructure is going to crumble. The Afghans will simply go back to their earlier system of having a minimum governmental presence. Capt Hall, "that earlier system was very ineffective; they have been mentored on how to make things effective, how to increase yield and production, how to manage the *Tashkil* (staffing) and all aspects of having an effecting government. The problem is that everything is based on traditions in Afghanistan. They plan on keeping it the way it was for their parents, grandparents, great grandparents, all the way up to the Persian Empire time period. Many times I have to tell people that Afghanistan is not America; just because we do something that works for us in America doesn't mean we have the right to force it down the Afghan throats and say you must do this. In the end it's their choice; if they want to revert back to their traditions and old ways, its up to them. It is not our position to tell the Afghan people and GIRoA what to do".

Afghan elders listened very carefully to officials from USAID and USDA who proposed that we want to establish a chamber of commerce for you so that the local businesses can effectively communicate with businesses at the national level. This is a great idea in theory but it's terrible for a war torn country like Afghanistan. The Linguist had issues translating "chamber of commerce"; after a while the elders said "We got it; tell us what kind of *kumak* you can provide us? This term loosely translates to 'assistance' but in the Afghan context it simply means "how much money you can give us". The elders did not sense any *kumak* coming their way and therefore left the *shura* without even eating the food.

Not everyone is appreciative of the developmental activities in Afghanistan. The Chief *Mullah* at a Kandahar mosque told me that they don't need all these developmental activities, especially schools, built by the CF "We don't know what these Marines are feeding our kids and we don't know what they are teaching our kids" said the Chief *Mullah*. They only need large madrassas, he asked me to convey his message to CF to fund madrassas. The Chief *Mullah* was very apprehensive of the real intention of the CF and especially the US forces. The *Mullah*s in the region I spoke to were of the opinion that the US has ulterior motives in staying in Afghanistan. "They ….the Americans….are after our Islam, they want to destroy Islam, they are killing our religious students, they are destroying our religious institutions. They….the Americans…..are only building schools, especially girl schools, we don't need girl schools, we only need madrassas, huge madrassas" said Molvi Abdul Rehman.

Development takes place in a cultural context and tribal societies in general are averse to haste in developmental activities. Afghanistan's tribal society is no different than other tribalized cultures and offers an impediment to development "There are a lot of tribal wars amongst themselves; I have witnessed lots and lots of land disputes, there is not a day goes by when someone comes to us with a complain about his land being occupied by someone else. There are no records and there is no way to prove such claims. If one person wanted a well here, someone else would complain and say they want a well at another location and it was a constant struggle and a constant battle with the very people whose lives we want to make better and their life more comfortable. Once people saw us doing something positive for them, then they would come and negotiate with us for more well projects; and then it got to a point where it was like give me, give me give all the time to a point where the Afghans are now asking for non-stop. When you tell then I can't do that or I don't have the funds to do that then they get all angry and accuse us of being out there all for ourselves, which is not true. We have poured billions and billions of dollars in this country. I don't think that they are fully of what we have gone through in terms of our country and our finances and all the losses we have taken so far, I don't think the Afghans fully appreciate that" said Capt Hall.

A classic case of misdirected development efforts was building a motor cycle repair and training facility at Now Zad District which notoriously became known as the "Now Zad Choppers". The idea was conceived by C-9 division of USMC at Camp Leatherneck. More than a million USD of tax payers' money was spent on a concrete building to house a motor cycle repair facility and provide vocational training in mechanical engineering (Photos 52. 53). Motor cycle mechanics refused to move to the new building as it was far away from the secure District center. The idea was so ill-conceived that the DG had to find an alternative use for the building. Eventually it will be converted into a personal abode. Similarly a new DG's compound and police stations were built for millions of dollars in the middle of nowhere (Photo 54). In Afghan context, security is everything and if a building cannot be secured, it cannot be utilized. Another example was the purchase of an ambulance for the local health center which was established and maintained by Bangladesh Rural Advancement Committee (BRAC). The CAG team leader during 2010-11 purchased a van which was converted into an ambulance at a cost of 16,000 USD. It was later revealed that the doctor at the BRAC clinic forged the registration documents for the van as it was a stolen vehicle. GIRoA could not produce new documents for the ambulance and it remained parked in the DG's compound for several years. Eventually, DG's bodyguard started using it as a house for his well-trained rooster! (Photos 55-58). Ghulam Habib, a high school senior, pocketed 5000 USD which he received as a micro-grant to establish a computer teaching center in Lashkar Gah.

Photo 52: "Now Zad Choppers" building in the middle of nowhere (under construction).

Photo 53: Completed "Now Zad Choppers" building in the middle of nowhere.

Photo 54: Bridge to Nowhere! Two large buildings are being constructed in the middle of nowhere in Helmand Province.

Photo 55: Stolen vehicle worth 16,000 USD as ambulance parked in the DG's compound.

Photo 56: A US Marine is posing with the ambulance being used as a rooster house.

Photo 57: A rooster is enjoying his comfortable abode.

Photo 58: Dr. Ibrahim posing with US Marines after receiving the final installment of funds for his "ambulance" project.

PRTs ROLE IN DEVELOPMENT

The overarching goal of reconstruction and development in Afghanistan was to "win the hearts and minds" of ordinary Afghans. How can you win the hearts and minds when nobody in Afghanistan has achieved that feat so far? "There is little empirical evidence that supports the assumption that reconstruction assistance is an effective tool to "win hearts and minds," and improve security or stabilization in counterinsurgency contexts (Feinstein and Wilder, 2012).

Reconstruction and development was mainly conducted by Provincial Reconstruction Teams (PRTs). There are 25 PRTs in Afghanistan under the authority of ISAF out of which 12 are led by the United States. PRTs at the provincial level are loosely connected to DSTs at the District level. PRTs have become an integral part of peacekeeping and stability operations; but they have also been criticized for their mixed effectiveness, over-emphasis on military objectives and priorities, failure to effectively coordinate and communicate with the UN and non-governmental organizations (NGOs), and differences in staffing and mission (Abbaszadeh et al, 2008).

The role of PRTs is highly questionable in the Afghan context. They delivered in very few situations and in most cases they proved either ineffective or counter-productive. In some cases, they implemented projects which negatively impacted the BSO. They implemented Quick Impact Projects (QIPs) and most of the money ended up in personal pockets. "The principal argument against QIPs was that projects were not sustainable, particularly where a project was delivered outside of government institutions and processes. The differences of opinion on the role of QIPs in generating consent and "force protection benefits" resulted in powerful controversies within the PRT, not least because the assumption of these benefits had organizational and tactical implications (Gordon, 2011).

Research has shown that there is no definitive relationship between unemployment and violence. Consequently, it may be misguided to seek political stability through short-term job creation in Afghanistan. "...... development funds are likely to buy more 'no-bang for the buck' when directed at small-scale projects that improve the quality of local government services, thereby inducing noncombatants to share intelligence about insurgents with their government and its allies" (Berman et al, 2011).

Coalition Forces have always compensated the Afghans for any damage caused to life or property as a result of their actions. On the other hand, Taliban have caused far more damage to Afghanistan than CF, but Afghans have never demanded compensation from them. Afghans do not like it when CF cause even the slightest damage to their property or crops. In one instance an Afghan demanded 1500 USD for a dead goat. They demand compensation for the entire crop field even if an armored vehicle has driven through a corner of the field and caused a minor damage to the crop.

One US Marine Lt. Col. referred to it as the "The Battle Damage Scam" referring to compensation claims for wheat field destruction, structural damages, and animal damages. "This is their country, this is their war and they should be a part of it and play their role. If we keep on paying them, it will eventually end up in Taliban's hands. Corn fields are the most favorite hiding places for Taliban fighters. If we stop paying them these hefty amounts for minor damages, the locals will simply ask the Taliban to stop fighting on their soil or homes" he said. But fact of the matter is that the ordinary Afghans never considered it as their own war, they always considered it a war between Taliban and *"Kharijis"* (NATO). As long as they don't own this war, peace in

Afghanistan will remain a distant reality. Wars cannot be won if the local population plays a neutral role.

Chapter 14
US/NATO Departure On The Horizon

The Afghan war is finally coming to an end in 2014. It has been marked by a series of shifting and unrealizable goals from installing democracy to promoting economic and social development, to battling drugs. The Lisbon meeting in late 2010 paved the way for NATO withdrawal by the end of 2014. NATO and its allies are faced with the ardent task of leaving Afghanistan. US is faced with pressure from home front to leave as quickly as possible and don't leave behind any forces. The ground realities in Afghanistan are so fragile that a complete withdrawal will lead to more chaos. However, leaving behind a small number of forces will render them more susceptible to insurgent attacks. As of late 2013, the US is mulling a residual force of 9000 to train the Afghan forces. The most important question everyone is asking is how stable the Afghan government is and whether ANSF can defend the country from being completely overrun by Taliban and other insurgents.

Gray (2011) argued that GIRoA is not capable of sustaining itself "Presiding over a territory that has never been ruled by a modern state, the Afghan government is not much more than a funnel for endemic corruption. In the event of a full-scale pull-out of US-led forces, it would be lucky to survive for more than 48 hours". *Mullah* Omar, the supreme leader of Taliban, announced in mid-2013 that they will take control of Kabul within two weeks of the NATO planned pull out in 2014. This statement might be an exaggeration but it certainly points to the impending turbulent time ahead. On the other side of DL, the question of ISI and its control over the Taliban insurgency is not fully understood by the decision makers.

"However, as the provider of sanctuary, and very substantial financial, military and logistical support to the insurgency, the ISI appears to have strong strategic and operational influence – reinforced by coercion. There is thus a strong case that the ISI and elements of the military are deeply involved in the insurgent campaign, and have powerful influence over the Haqqani network" (Waldman, 2010).

There are real concerns about the stability of Afghan government after the US fully withdraws majority of its forces. Afghanistan is faced with major challenges, from security, to corruption, to terrorism and most of all a lack of national identity. Historically, that has always been the case but the intra-tribal rivalries have reached unprecedented levels. Despite the fact that Karzai tried to make some efforts towards national reconciliation, most tribes are not happy with him "……even his clothes preached integration, from his silky green Northern *chappan* (cloak) to his Pashtun sandals – but his government has been characterized by ethnic rivalry. With Karzai reaching out to the mainly Pashtun Taliban for peace talks, and surrounding himself in the presidency with Pashtuns, many Tajiks, Uzbeks, Turkmens, and Hazaras are starting to look to their own ethnic groups for leadership" (Baldauf, 2012).

This simply implies that without a change in Pakistani behavior it will be nearly impossible for US and its NATO allies to leave the Afghan government on its own. As has been recently exposed in the Doha peace process, the ISI support is undisputed in bringing Taliban to the negotiating table. The international community is finding it increasingly difficult to treat Pakistan as an effective partner and ally. The US Congressional reports indicate that since the war began, the US has provided Pakistan with 11.6 billion USD in security-related assistance and 6 billion USD in economic aid (Kronstadt, 2010a and b). However, the newspaper reports based on leaked papers from Edward Snowden show that the US has given out 26 billion USD to Pakistan. This could be a staggering amount for an ally which has not been very trustworthy in recent years. According to the 'Enhanced Partnership with Pakistan Act 2009', the US is due to dish out at least 7.5 billion USD of aid over the next five years.

While leaving the scene, the US has to closely watch the conduct of Pakistan and its spy agency (ISI). The challenge is to face an unstable, nuclear-armed country that faces a serious internal threat from extremist groups inside Pakistan, some of which are supported by the Pakistani establishment. Nonetheless, Pakistan has long been suspected of playing a double-game of astonishing magnitude. "The conflict has led to the deaths of over 1,000 American and 700 other foreign military personnel; thousands of Afghan soldiers, police, officials and civilians; and an unknown number of Afghan, Pakistani and other foreign insurgents. It has already cost America nearly 300 billion USD, and now costs over 70 billion USD a year (Waldman, 2010). A Haqqani commander once put it: "Of course Pakistan is the main cause of the problems [in Afghanistan] but America is behind Pakistan".

NATO retrograde (Photo 59) will closely be following the Russian retrograde model and contacts have already been made with the Russian Defense Ministry asking for guidance. NATO will still be heavily dependent on the Pakistani land route as the only viable, economic option. In the past, NATO convoys passing through Pakistani territory have come under attacks from the Pakistani hardliners. The political landscape in Khyber Pukhtunkhwa (KP) Province adjoining the Afghan border has changed and some religio-political parties have asked the government to completely ban these convoys. The anti-American sentiment in Pakistan is the highest since war in Afghanistan began in late 2001.

Photo 59: A New Dawn; NATO tanks on their way out from northern Helmand (March 2011).

The larger question is hanging over everybody's head "What should be done to prevent this country from falling back into the hands of Taliban and Al-Qaeda?" I asked Capt Hall who served on several occasions in Afghanistan. "that's a very difficult question because we will always be fighting terrorism for the rest of our lives. I feel that when America pull out of here, we will be going somewhere else fighting terrorists. There is really no way I see in this world to 100% get rid of terrorist groups. It's just a simple fact that we Americans or the Britons or Danes can't afford to spend the rest of our lives and try to uphold other peoples' properties that they should be picking a stand on. If the government of Afghanistan is not willing to be strong enough to stand up to terrorists; It's up to the Afghan government and Afghan people, we have done what we can. We sacrificed so much over here, both in terms of money and lives. I recently had a cousin who lost both of his legs and his arms here. So we know what it means to sacrifice and the American people have sacrificed. Afghanistan has to stand up as its own country; they need to develop strong leadership and they have to develop a basic trust among the local populace to stand up to the Taliban and overthrow them. They still like the Taliban government and say that there were much less IEDs and killings but that was still not the way to live. Until Afghans decides to stand up to Taliban and keep them out, there is nothing the international community can do to protect them. The international forces cannot stay here forever to help protect them. Capt. Hall believes "After 9/11 we realized that we need to take the fight to the enemy. We came here to support the Afghan people against the oppression of Taliban".

Capt. Hall went on to describe the behavior of ordinary Afghans about the war on terror "When you ask the ordinary Afghans about the decade-old war, they say it's between Taliban and ISAF, we are not a part of it and we have nothing to do with it, we are just silent spectators. At the most they will say we don't know if we are with the ISAF or Taliban; they will say they are playing a neutral role".

If the Afghans are not a part of this war then one wonders who are these insurgents fighting with ISAF for the past ten years. The western observers often ask the question; where is the military-age segment of the population? A cursory look at the civilian population gives us an insight; we either see children under the age of 11 or adults older than 45 years of age (Photos 60-63). Anyone in between is either working directly or indirectly for this insurgency. This segment of the population is their sons, brothers, fathers and relatives. There is no doubt that a large number of these fighters are supplied by ISI and jihadi groups from across the border in Pakistan.

Photo 60: Little girls running a grocery store in northern Helmand (February 2012).

Photo 61: Fun times; A US Marine is hands up to a little kid with a toy gun (October 2011).

Photo 62: Grand Bargain; A teenager is trying to exchange his cell phone for the shades.

Photo 63: Afghans love for Martial Arts continues even during a bloody war (Now Zad, 2012).

When the Afghan people do not consider Taliban as their enemy, how come the international community can win this war? "They [the Afghan population] are supporting the Taliban and they don't want to see their sons and relatives get killed. The Afghan people may not like what the Taliban are doing but they are not openly against it. Whether they openly admit or not, but doing nothing against the Taliban is telling me that they are supporting them. You really can't be neutral in a situation like this. I don't think that you can stand by and watch being killed, injured or maimed for life and be fine with that. Quite frankly, it upsets me when you look at people do nothing about it and then they complain to us" remarked Capt. Hall.

I asked a former provincial Governor (who declined to be named) about the transition to GIRoA. ISAF has announced a withdrawal timetable and USMC will soon be leaving Helmand. In your opinion, is this a positive step? "Absolutely, this is a very good step. Let me give you examples of those Districts where peace and security has been established such as Marjah, Nawa and Garam Ser; police in these Districts move about freely and people have come to the GIRoA fold. They [Taliban] cannot dare to come there. The expenditure in other Districts to maintain ISAF should be diverted to the local governments. If half or even one fourth of the ISAF spending is diverted to the District governments, there will be a lot of developmental work; they will be happy and we will be happy! In less secure Districts such as Kajaki, Now Zad and Washer, they should speed up the transition so that local governments start functioning and employ more ALP as it has been hugely successful in other Districts" he responded.

There have been two opposing views on the US pullout from Afghanistan; one segment of Afghan society believes "a swift pullout will lead to the collapse of the Afghan government, the breakup of the national army, and the spark of a new civil war. Still, the past decade hasn't been a waste, many Afghans say" (Baldauf, 2012). However, the Taliban sympathizers strongly believe that the US should have pulled out a long time ago. They argue that the current violence in the region is a direct consequence of the NATO intervention in their country. Either way, the future of Afghanistan and hence the entire region appears to be in a limbo.

Zalmay, age 45 and an Ishaqzai, who was a former *Mujahideen* commander said "We have to finish this war ourselves, unless we stop fighting, these 45 nations who are currently in Afghanistan can never end this war". Ahmadullah, age 34 from Kandahar served as a local contractor for ISAF. He grew up in both Afghanistan and Pakistan and was responsible for providing internet connectivity on coalition bases. He strongly believes that *Mullah* Omar is hiding in Pakistan as the CF has searched any possible hideouts inside Afghanistan. Ahmadullah put the entire blame on Pakistan for all the woes in Afghanistan.

Everybody is scratching their heads as to what is the best way to get out of Afghanistan and how to stabilize the nascent Afghan government. The western powers are determined to "impose" democracy on a tribalized society. "In the blind rush to export an idealized version of western governance, it has been forgotten that democracy comes in several versions, some of them highly illiberal. If a functioning democracy were to develop in Afghanistan in the current conditions, it would most likely be a variant of the Rousseau type that exists in Iran. The effect could be to entrench the power of the Taliban" (Gray, 2011).

Chapter 15
MISSED OPPORTUNITIES

The case of Now Zad District in Helmand Province is presented here as an example of how defeat can be snatched from the jaws of success! In the backdrop of the Afghan war in late 2011, Helmand Province was relatively quiet after the Taliban were pushed out to the east towards Qandahar. It was my understanding that this push was part of the "Squeeze" policy where on the one hand Taliban were being flushed out towards the Pakistani border by the international forces and on the other hand they were being pushed towards the west presumably by the Pakistani forces. The larger mission at Now Zad FOB was to clear the remaining pockets of Taliban and help establish a complete control of the District administration. CAG (Photo 64) was especially entrusted with the task to help the Now Zad District administration (Photo 65) re-establish and reassert itself and stand on its feet, a monumental task in a country ravaged by war for the better part of the last four decades.

Their main objective was to create a stable environment for GIRoA to succeed and peace will endure after their departure (in 2014). Capt Petit and his CAG team was very supportive of GIRoA in the northern Helmand District of Now Zad which has witnessed some of the fierce fighting starting from the *Mujahideen* era. The British bombed this area and destroyed a large number of civilian structures. "We only had a general understanding of the situation but we didn't have a very good sense of what we were expected of or what we are going to achieve here in northern Helmand. Although the Helmand Plan provided a general guideline, we had to figure things out on our own" said Capt Petit. "People tend to have a hard time grasping the concept of a community, they are largely driven by their self-interest". "They are survivors and they can make good of meager resources".

This Civil Affairs team greatly digressed from their predecessors and adopted a development model which was based on the needs of the local communities. Instead of stuffing money into GIRoA and their favorites, they assessed the needs of the people and through a fair selection process, awarded small contracts which directly helped the BSO. This CAG empowered the DG, and asked the locals to contact their government officials rather than wait in line at the military base and PRT.

There were a number of missed opportunities in terms of achieving the Coalition objectives through less violent means. For example, the Taliban shadow government in Bar Now Zad (Upper Now Zad) was never approached to join the GIRoA, rather Special Ops were conducted, and those too without the knowledge of the local BSO. The Weapons Company of 2nd Battalion 4th Marine Regiment (2/4) decided to engage the low level Taliban operatives in the southern part of their AO, rather than approach their leadership in Bar Now Zad. The botched effort resulted in several injuries to the CF and the loss of a brilliant Marine Sgt William C. Stacey. The Company was trying to move the 'Line in the sand' by expanding the 'Security Bubble' they have wrapped around themselves.

Photo 64: The author with a group of US Marines (October, 2011).

Photo 65: Mayor Juma Khan looking at his renovated Bazar (December, 2011).

One USMC commander I spoke to put it this way "We have a tendency to be interested in, attracted to and focused on things which are exciting instead of things which are boring. We are more interested in fighting the enemy, finding caches of arms and ammunition and heroin-making factories. We believe that if we find and kill the bad guys and destroy the drugs, then we will achieve our over-arching objectives".

It appears as if the CF got distracted in achieving strategic over-arching objective which is to leave behind a stable and self-sustaining Afghanistan. "We got bogged down with fighting and killing so much that we forgot the alternatives; figuring out the infrastructure issues, mentoring the GIRoA, effectively managing projects, information operations, ARRP and training the ANSF which is a lot less attractive than going on patrols and fighting the Taliban". Not only the CF, but the media is also interested in exciting things rather than important things. "We sometimes forget that we are here to do a job and not be entertained or to have fun or to get into adrenaline rush. It may be a failure on part of the leadership to clearly convey to people throughout the ranks what is it exactly that we are trying to achieve. I have seen some strange risk calculations; it is perfectly acceptable to go out and diffuse IEDs and conduct operations at the periphery of the security bubble, but it's not ok to take interest in the District center. We know the environment, we know the people and we know it's safe with a low risk of IEDs, but somebody who has spent little time here is incharge of risk calculation. There appears to be a lack of trust in the people who are operating at the lower level and who can better understand the kinetics and even non-kinetic environments". In most cases the local commanders were not allowed to make low-level basic decisions.

Chapter 16
THE WAY FORWARD

AMERICAN LEGACY IN AFGHANISTAN

"A decade ago, playing music could get you maimed in Afghanistan. Today, a youth ensemble is traveling to the Kennedy Center and Carnegie Hall. And it even includes girls."
(Washington Post, February 3, 2013)

In 2003, a significant shift took place in the Afghan war. The US military diverted its attention to overthrow Saddam from Power in Iraq. It was important for the then Administration to punish Saddam for his Kuwait offensive. The Weapons of Mass Destruction saga need not be elaborated here and is beyond the scope of this book, but interested readers are referred to publications on this topic elsewhere. The US military applied its full force in overthrowing Saddam and this objective was achieved with little loss of lives on the US side.

This caused a significant drain on military resource availability in Afghanistan. This proved to be the beginning of a new chapter for Al Qaeda. For the next five years Afghanistan remained on life support in terms of the US involvement. Iraq suddenly became the cornerstone of the US Middle East policy. The nascent government of Hamid Karzai was left on its own and for the terrorists this was a perfect opportunity to reorganize and regroup. The neo-conservatives in the US strongly believed that removing Saddam was more important than dismantling terror networks in Afghanistan and lawless FATA. They also firmly believed that the Iraq war will pay for itself as the US will get enough oil out of the region. We all know how that adventure turned out!

The two concurrent wars in Afghanistan and Iraq put a heavy drain on the American economy and many economists are of the opinion that the economy went into recession as a result of these adventures. "We have been waging war with an ATM that has run out of cash. We must implement a strategy that matches our reduced means. Being poorer, we have to fight smarter" (West, 2011). Iraq is in the worst shape since the departure of Saddam Hussein and the stability of Afghanistan is in question as well. Being one of the worst dictators of modern history, Saddam managed to keep the nation intact. IT appears as if exporting democracy to Iraq didn't work well for its tribalized structure.

When US President Barak Obama was elected to office in 2008, he vowed to end both the Iraq and Afghan wars. He made good on his promise regarding Iraq, but ending the Afghan war proved difficult than was originally thought. President Obama decided to make one last push in the Afghan war, and just like Iraq, he initiated a 'troop surge' for Afghanistan in 2009. This strategy pushed the Taliban away but did not completely eliminate the insurgents' threat to Karzai's inefficient government. After a heavy loss of life on the American side, the Coalition Forces will finally withdraw at the end of 2014.

In essence, there were many occasions in the past 13 years to end the Afghan war and declare victory but it's never too late to end it now. The best time to scale down the war arrived when Karzai government was installed in 2004 but the US did not avail that opportunity and walked into the trap Al Qaeda had intricately laid down in the Afghan mountains. DoD and USAID remained heavily involved in 'nation building' spending billions of dollars (Photo 66). The good news is that not all this money ended up in banks in Dubai, though it heavily contributed to the Afghan corruption.

Photo 66: A USAID official is having an informal chat with Afghan children in Now Zad (October 2011).

Recent polls show that most Americans do not have a favorable view of the situation in Afghanistan. They believe that they went into Afghanistan with the wrong expectations; Americans thought that they would change their beliefs, culture and actually form a democratic government. Most Americans I spoke to believe that Afghanistan will revert back to its old ways of tribal warfare and not much has changed in the last 13 years. However, some war veterans believe that Afghanistan is a humanitarian success; schools are being built and women are gaining more rights.

The most obvious change we see in today's Afghanistan is rapid urbanization. It is still not clear if this is because of the policies implemented by the Coalition partners or the returning refugees are also playing a part in it. According to USAID reports, about 50% of the population now lives in cities and towns. This number maybe highly exaggerated as an average of 28% of the population lives in urban centers in the entire South Asian region. Kabul is the only 'mega' city in the country with five million people which is a 5-fold increase since the Taliban regime left the scene in 2002. Similarly, the populations of Farah, Herat, Jalalabad and Kandahar have all tripled in the past decade. It is believed that urbanization will eventually weaken ethnic and tribal affiliations and help women to get better employment and education opportunities.

Afghans are increasingly being plugged into the global grid and about 70% of the population has now access to mobile phones. There are frequent voice and data outages and in most rural areas, data connectivity is not available altogether. This is still far better than eight years ago when there were virtually no mobile phone users in the entire country.

David Ignatius (2013) argues that Afghanistan has made significant improvements in all sectors since the war began in 2001. "The urbanization and economic development that have reshaped Afghanistan do not mean that the country will have a bright political future or that the Taliban won't regain a measure of power after U.S. troops leave in 2014. But the future won't simply be a replay of the past. The Afghanistan movie won't just restart where it left off when the Taliban were driven from power".

Significant strides have been taken to improve infrastructure and education. A large number of schools and professional institutions have sprung in the urban centers; though rural population is still missing these amenities. Prospects of a well-developed mineral sector has attracted a large number of geoscience professionals from the neighboring countries.

Over the course of 13 years, American military and civilian personnel have developed great friendships with their Afghan counterparts (Photo 67). Despite the occasional "Green on Blue" attacks, the two militaries have developed a greater understanding and cooperation. This can certainly be regarded as a positive outcome of the long Afghan war.

Photo 67: Green on Blue friendship: An AUP cop with his Marine buddy (November 2011).

REGIONAL SOLUTION

"Our mistake in Afghanistan was to do the work of others for ten years, expecting reciprocity across a cultural and religious divide" West, Bing (2011)

When it comes to finding a lasting solution, Afghanistan is NOT an international issue; it is only a regional conflict. After the defeat of Al-Qaeda, the foreign troops must have exited as soon possible. That did not happen and we see a worsening security situation in the country. The "Pakistan" and "Iran" issues must be solved first in order to bring a relative peace to Afghanistan. The two long, unstable borders of Pakistan (with Afghanistan and India) have created more issues in south Asian region than any other factor.

A cursory look at Afghan history reveals that the only people who can manage Afghanistan are the Afghans themselves. They don't respond favorably to any foreign intervention; whether it's Pakistan imposing Taliban on them or the US trying to impose democracy on them, until Afghans agree that this is what they want. "The history of Afghanistan is that invaders and conventional forces invariably lose in the end. Just as the Russians did, the west faces a determined insurgency, financed from abroad and inspired by Islamist fundamentalism. The Taliban, with an endless supply of recruits from the madrasas across the frontier in Pakistan, could fight for ever. Taking ground is much easier than holding it" (Lyon, 2008).

A regional solution is the only way to solve the four decade old Afghan quagmire. Initially, the international community should back off and let the Afghans decide their own future. 'Leave it to them, let them fight it out' is the dictum of the tribalized societies. Iran needs to be brought back into the mainstream international politics and it appears as if the recent elections of 2013 have brought forth a pragmatic Iranian leadership. The tentative agreement on Iran's nuclear ambitions in late 2013 is a step in the right direction. Iran is desperate to play its role as a regional power and the US must accommodate Iran's apprehensions vis-à-vis Israel and Saudi Arabia.

Pakistan must be stabilized; the country is on a dangerous collision path and it will soon be imploding. The sectarian conflict between the majority Sunni and minority Shia Islamists is at its peak and it is one of the many factors which will have a spillover effect. The Kashmir issue is currently on the back burner and it must be resolved before any lasting peace can be expected between India and Pakistan; the two nuclear neighbors. Currently, there is a much bigger problem in Pakistan than in Afghanistan. Just like many other regional players, India and Pakistan are fighting a proxy war on the Afghan soil. Once these regional issues are taken care of, then the international community can initiate a limited engagement starting with education and healthcare. The life expectancy in Afghanistan is only 44 years!

The sobering picture inside Afghanistan is crying out loud for a regional solution. The Afghan military is fragile and highly dependent on outside support. There is an unofficial 40% unemployment and therefore no dearth of recruits for the Taliban. The madrassas across the border in Pakistan are churning immense numbers of young Islamists who are ready to fight the "infidels" and die. Terrorist attacks are on the rise and schools and healthcare facilities are being targeted. The atmosphere of disappointment and bitterness has continued to plague the Afghans since 1973.

There is no need to 'stay behind' in Afghanistan to train the ANSF. Afghan soldiers can be moved to a third country such as Germany or Turkey and trained there.

Roberts (2009) painted the following picture about the upcoming situation in the country. "The present campaign in Afghanistan is unlikely to result in a clear victory for the Kabul government and its outside partners, because the sources of division within and around Afghanistan are just too deep, and the tendency to react against the presence of foreign forces too ingrained. The war could yet be lost, or, perhaps more likely, it could produce a stalemate or a long war of attrition with no clear outcome. The dissolution of Afghanistan into regional fiefdoms – already an accustomed part of life – could continue and even accelerate". If this happens, it will further push the world closer to an all-out war.

This gloomy picture continued to evolve and Gray (2011) predicted the following; "It is hard to imagine any kind of democracy in Afghanistan in the foreseeable future. In the event of a full drawdown of western forces, a many-sided civil war would ensue and the hapless peoples of Afghanistan would face a future without effective government, democratic or otherwise. Again, the underlying problem is political rather than military. There can be no peace in Afghanistan for as long as it is used as a theatre to play out regional conflicts".

In the above mentioned scenario, then what are the chances for a lasting peace in the region? "The near-term prospects for security and political reconciliation in Afghanistan are bleak. Nonetheless, the United States, its coalition partners, and neighboring states can still assist in shaping sustainable, Afghan-led stabilization, in accordance with their overlapping national interests" (Chorev and Sherman, 2010).

Hadley and Podesta (2012) argued "any political solution to the conflict in Afghanistan will be sustainable only if it forms part of a larger regional settlement. The Pakistanis, in particular, need to come on board and may require some U.S. prodding to get there.

Pakistan has undermined the prospects for long-term peace in Afghanistan by providing sanctuary, training, and financial support to the insurgency, in part to counter what it fears will be undue Indian influence in the country".

The four decades of war and unrest has left Afghanistan more backward than it would have been under normal circumstances. Civil, political and military institutions are in shambles and need major overhaul. Afghanistan is now home to an entire generation of illiterate adults. It is now surrounded by rapidly developing countries such as China, India and Iran. So far Afghanistan was the focus of the global war on terror and therefore all the major global and regional actors were interested in its reconstruction. Gleason et al. (2009) puts it this way; "Afghanistan's tragic history of occupation, external domination, exploitation, disorder and disarray calls for broad-based and widely regional support for reconstruction".

There is a strong need for a regional dialogue on the Afghan crisis. The international community should not only facilitate such a dialogue but also make sure that concrete steps are taken to avoid further destabilization of a region where nuclear arsenal could end up in the hands of the *Jihadi* terrorists.

THE ELUSIVE FUTURE

Every society goes through a natural evolutionary process and, therefore, a society cannot be transformed overnight. The process of societal evolution in Afghanistan was going forward at its normal pace until 1973. The natural course has been completely overturned since then. The Russians and Americans have tried to change the course of the entire Afghan history.

Multiple complex layers have been added onto this fluid situation in the past four decades; religious fundamentalism being one of them. Afghan society is one of many tribal societies which lay at the bottom of the pyramid in terms of societal evolution; the advanced nations being at the top. I asked the District Governor of Zaranj in Nimroz Province as to what he thinks of the future for his country. "Our major dilemma is how to separate our own from the others; those folks whose strings are pulled from somewhere else. One major element in this [equation] is Taliban. If, God willing, Taliban decided to be a part of the [peace] process, then it will not take more than 3 months [for the peace to prevail]. I am hopeful that this reconciliation will take place soon and it is a major issue; smaller obstacles along the road can be taken care of easily. Foreigners have a major role in this process and also God has his own designs for us, so I can't say anything about it".

Plenty of failed policies have been implemented in Afghanistan to warn future decision makers. The US policy of disengagement in the 1990s and massive briberies in the 2000s have led to disastrous results. "There is no alternative to an incremental, trial-and-error approach, stressing effective feedback that reflects the nuances of Afghan realities rather than what the decision makers want to hear" (Isby, 2011).

It has been called the 'wrong war' by Bing West and other leading defence and political analysts. "We have fought the wrong war with the wrong strategy. Our troops are not a Peace Corps; they are fighters" (West, 2011). To some observers, Afghanistan often seems like a country where nothing ever changes and the same story of ethnic and tribal struggle repeats itself in an endless loop. However, hopelessness is not in the best interest of any party entagled in the Afghan web. if all waring factions, internal and external, pull back from their positions and let the common Afghans decide their fate, it may not take that much time time to convert this elusive future into a certain future!

In order to achieve this objective, the Afghan leadership has to come forward and accept the enormous responsibility of steering their nation into the 21st century. Blaming others for their own failures will drag this conflict indefinitely. The Afghans have suffered enormously at the hands of their own kith and kin and it is time to heal some of the wounds and provide solace to the millions of war orphans and widows.

Enough blood has already been spilled on the Afghan soil; its now time to give peace a chance. There are plenty of examples around the world where nations have stepped back from the brink of destruction and have carved a path of peace and reconciliation for themselves in a short amount fo time. Northern Ireland, Sri Lanks, South Africa, and Angola are all examples of countries with successful peace processes. Ferocious armed groups in these countries have laid down their arms and joined the mainstream political systems.

The government of Nelson Madela constituted a comission for 'truth and reconciliation' in South Africa after they abolished the apartheid. A commision along those lines may be a viable option for a short-term solution and can be used as a necessary exercise to enable Afghans to reconcile with their past on a morally accepted basis and to advance the cause of national rebuilding and prosperity.

In the long run, Afghans have to decide for themselves as to what is in their best interest. They can choose between tribalism and modern education. They lie at the bottom of almost every international index and equipping themselves with modern education is the only way out of the abyss in which they find themselves in the 21st century.

The year 2014 is a significant milestone not only for the international stakeholders in Afghanistan but for the Afghans themselves. It will soon be determined how many foreign troops would the Afghans allow to state in their country beyond 2014, but it would be insignificant in the long run. Afghans must determine their own future and prepare to stand on their own feet as they are sitting on a pot of Gold. It is entirely up to them if they want to convert it into a golden opportunity or a golden curse. The international community must facilitate the Afghans transition from a Cold War mind set to the realities of the tech-dominant 21st century. It is in the best interest of everyone to have a stable Afghanistan.

APPENDIX – A
Beginnings

It was a hot summer morning in Hattiesburg, MS when I finally decided to say goodbye to my academic career for good. I had several options for my next career, but I decided to take the one which was unorthodox, adventurous, far away from home and possibly lethal. No, I was not going to find the lost tribe in the Amazon jungle, nor I was on the hunt for Atlantis! I was headed to Afghanistan.

It was to give a serious thought to become a DoD contractor for the US military fighting the longest war of its history in Afghanistan. Little I knew that this would become a complete 180 degree turn from what I had been doing all my life since college. The only career I knew till this date was academics and scholarly activities related to my beloved profession; being a Himalayan Geologist.

I was issued 3 duffle bags full of army gear and I was told that you have to carry it all without any assistance! I guess the army folks don't know that these days the airlines are contemplating to charge a fee even for a small carry-on bag. The IOTV (Improved Outer Tactical Vest) alone was more than 40 lbs! Don't be confused, it's the military acronym for a bullet-proof vest. The combined weight of the gear was close to 200 lbs, not including my personal belongings.

A chartered plane dropped me off at the scorching heat of Kuwait city where I was guided to a transient tent. The 130 degree F temperatures kept me away from paying too much attention to my surroundings. After spending five days at Kuwait City, I arrived at the Bagram Air Base (BAF) which is the largest base for ISAF in Afghanistan. I was assigned to Helmand Province and arrived at Camp Leatherneck (LNK) a week after my arrival at BAF. LNK is located is the middle of Regestan which is a literal translation for a desert. This desert extends from southern Pakistan to the Afghan Provinces of Qandahar and Helmand. I finally met my military POC (Point of Contact) and I was issued one more duffle bag of military gear, this time by the US Marines. From this point onwards, I was all over southern Afghanistan and would occasionally fly back to Kabul as well, the rest, as they say, is history!

APPENDIX - B
The Influence of Religion

Islam was introduced to the world around 590 AD at a time when idol worshipping was very common and people have largely forgotten the teachings of the last widespread religion of Christianity. The three main religions have all been introduced to the land of Arabia (loosely called the Middle East). Three Holy books accompanied the three main religions; Holy Torah, Bible and Quran which "descended" in that order. The world has not seen any new and widespread religion with a global appeal in the last 1500 years. According to repeated promises in the Holy Quran, Islam is the last religion until the Day of Judgment when the entire universe will collapse and all humans will be judged according to their worldly deeds. It probably refers to an antithesis of the Big Bang theory, as every system has a finite age.

The advent of Islam was an instant hit and it gained acceptance throughout Arabia, northern Africa, Balkans, and south and southeast Asia. This process was completed without any excessive bloodshed and it can be termed as a bloodless revolution. It took about 300 years to establish stable Islamic republics in all directions around Arabia.

As with its predecessor religion, the fall of Islam started after about 600 years of its existence around 1200 AD. Muslims rulers turned into monarchs and kings and despots and lost touch with their people. Justice system was the hallmark of all Muslim republics, and around the time of the fall of Islam, the justice system also went down the drain. Greed became more rampant and the rulers considered themselves above the law. Moral corruption started to creep into the ruling families. The general population remained pious, peaceful and pragmatic.

Islam was introduced to the Indian subcontinent in 712 AD when Muhammad Bin Qasim invaded India from the south through the Arabian Sea. He got limited success as his life was cut short in 715 AD by direct orders from his ruler in Arabia (Hujjaj Bin Yousaf) He was not very happy with Qasim's sudden rise of fame. Local people started to convert to Islam because Qasim was leading by example. He did not use any force for converting the local population to Islam.

Fast forward to 1526 when Zahiruddin Muhammad Babar attacked India from northwest (through Khyber Pass) and established one of the most successful dynasties called the Mughal Empire with capital at Delhi. Babar grew up in Central Asia, more specifically in Farghana (currently in eastern Uzbekistan). His successors ruled India until 1857 when British took over. Again they lost power for the same reason; conspiring against each other and not keeping up with the modern teachings. Islamic teachings have remained stagnant for the past about 500 years, though there is a very powerful in-built system in Islam where laws, rules and regulations are updated according to the research of the ones who know Islam.

Fast forward to post cold war scenario, where American foreign policy and interests are supreme and dictating and shaping up the present world. Osama Bin Laden (OBL) was heavily supported against the Russians and he turned against his western supporters right after the soviet defeat. Taliban and other terrorists were created and now no one knows how to control the situation where so many powerful players have met their ultimate demise. Saudis, Iranians, Indians, afghans, central Asians, Pakistanis, Chinese, Americans, Israelis and Russians, have all gathered in one tiny place around the Khyber Pass to battle out their proxies. Taliban and other fundamentalists are the current owners of Islam, let's see who will be the ultimate winners and losers this time around!

Pashtuns have always been misled by "Islam". In 1920, when Indian *Ulema* (religious scholars) declared the British India government illegal, they issued a fatwa asking Indian Muslims to migrate to an Islamic State. The Islam-loving Pashtuns from Peshawar and adjoining areas crossed the DL to Afghanistan and most of them were starved to death, they were returned by their Afghan brethren. The referendum of 1947 to decide the fate of Pashtun regions was heavily influenced by religion. In 1971, the Two-Nation theory fell apart and the Bengali Muslims declared their own independent state. The Martial Law of 1977 put this entire region on a path of utter destruction. General Zia was looking for legitimacy and the Soviet occupation of Afghanistan provided him with a golden opportunity. Islam again played a crucial role in destabilizing the region. The *Mujahideen* commanders left no stone unturned in destroying peace in Afghanistan after the Soviet withdrawal in 1989. Mullah Omar is still the *Amirul Momineen* and his rule will remain one of the darkest chapters in the recent Afghan history. We all know very well what happened to the brave Pashtuns of Swat and Dir when *Maulana* Sufi Muhammad ordered them to go to war against the infidels in Afghanistan in 2001.

Separation of church and state is not currently possible in the Islamic world. The case of Malaysian process is a success story.

They have limited the role of religion in politics and state and as a result have become a successful nation. On the contrary, the neighboring Indonesia is still reeling from religious fundamentalism and therefore still not making any economic progress. Same is the case for Philippines. Pashtuns are now so misguided that *Mullahs* (Taliban) are ruling them. They are converted into suicide bombers and are practically butchered by their masters on either side of the DL. Traditionally, *Mullah* had a very restricted role in a *Hujra*-dominated Pashtun society. Pashtuns can only come out of their shadowy life if they rally around open-minded Pashtuns, otherwise their very existence can be put in danger. There are some very strong foreign forces (especially Wahabis) who are actively working to destroy the fabric of Pashtun society and most Pashtuns take that as "Islam".

APPENDIX - C
The reality of a Pakistani Nation

Political scientists define the term 'Nation' as "a grouping of people who share real or imagined common history, culture, language or ethnic origin, often possessing or seeking its own government". I have been wondering whether this definition really fits to the Pakistani situation.

Historically, the territories which currently comprise Pakistan, have never shared a common origin. Until 1971, Pakistan had another component (presently Bangladesh) which was separated from its present portion by 1000 miles of the Indian soil. Historically, this entire region is India and Pakistan was carved out of it.

There are as many cultures in Pakistan, as there are people in it. Pakistan has four or five Provinces, a number of territories, an entire no-man's land called the FATA, and provincially administered tribal areas. Every Province has its own culture and then there are subcultures in every Province and every District and division. The role of women in society is as diverse as the color of Pakistani soils.

There are thousands of different languages spoken in various parts of the country. Every language is distinct from the other one and everyone thinks their language will take them to the heavens. Urdu (a variation of Hindi) was adopted as the so called national language but only 5% of the population speaks it as their first language and only 40% of the population understands it.

Ethnically, the country is divided along all possible lines. Pashtuns think that they are the superior of all the peoples of Pakistan. Punjabis are proud of their ethnic origin and look down upon Pashtuns, Sindhis are a totally different creed and Baluchis believe that their land has been occupied by Pakistan Army. There are thousands of other ethnic groups in every Province of the country.

The question is if they country is so diverse then what is holding them together? There is not much holding them together except the brutal force of the military rulers and police. The only binding force for the Pakistani "Nation" is their common religion. 95 % of the country is Muslim and the country is as divided on religious basis as on any other parameter. Sunnis, Shias, Ahmadis, Ahle-Hadis, Barelvi, etc. etc. all ready to cut each other's' throats because everyone thinks that they are the God- chosen ones and they have the keys to the heavens.

There are only two countries in the world which were created in the name/disguise of religion; Pakistan and Israel. Both of them are faced with existential threats. Time will tell as to who will emerge victorious in this epic battle.

APPENDIX - D
An Introduction to Now Zad District
Helmand Province (Capt. Michael C. Petit, USMC)

Now Zad District lies in the North West of Helmand Province, Afghanistan. Neighboring Districts to the east are Musa Qala, to the northeast Baghran, to the north is the Por Chaman and Golestan Districts in the Farah Province. South of Now Zad is Nahri Sarraj (NES) and to the west is Washir. A lowly populated area comprised of 16 major villages and more than 300 smaller villages, Now Zad is home to fertile farmland and territory valued highly by the Taliban. Over the last 30 years Now Zad has seen heavy fighting -- initially during the Communist era, the Soviet occupation, and subsequently the mujahedeen period that lasted from 1989-1996.

The Taliban ruled the area from 1996-2001, until they were forced to leave by the Northern Alliance, assisted by the US led coalition. In 2005-6 the local population reinforced by Taliban rose up against the local government, as a result of its brutality in particular towards the Ishaqzai tribe. Heavy fighting took place in 2006-7 with coalition forces fighting the insurgency in Now Zad District Centre, displacing up to 20,000 people to other areas in Now Zad, Gereshk, Lashkar Gah and even Pakistan. The majority of the people are still displaced, awaiting an improvement in the security and economic situation in order for them to return.

Many compounds in the DC were damaged as a result of the heavy fighting. In 2009 the USMC conducted a clearance operation in Now Zad District Centre (DC) and established a secure zone around the DC. These actions enabled some of the displaced people to return. Estimates of the population in Now Zad District vary starkly ranging from 36,000 to 108,000. Current estimates are that there are approximately 16,000 residents in the collection of villages termed the "District center area." This includes Alizai, Shekhzai, Deh Baluch, Damien, Changowlak, Barakzai, Karez Afghan, Khwaja Jamal, and Soorkano/Roshan Abad.

Now Zad is tribally heterogeneous, with significant populations of Alizai, Alikozai, Barakzai, Popalzai, Noorzai, Ishaqzai, Tajiks, Hazaras and more. The largest tribes of the District are Ishaqzai, Alikozai, Noorzai and Popalzai. Historically the Popalzai and Barakzai, who mainly resides in and around Now Zad DC, has been amongst the more Pro-GIRoA, with the Popalzai providing the many administrators in Now Zad. The current DCOP is of the Popalzai tribe who hub of power appears to be in the Kushk/Jihazai area.

The Ishaqzai, who resides mainly to the north, e.g. Bar Now Zad, and south (Georgian AO) of the DC, are generally seen as anti-GIRoA, along with the Noorzai (reside mostly in the south – the key elders is Hajji Rangin Khan of Kurghay). They constitute a significant part of the local Taliban. Due to the displacement of the people, the tribes have become more mixed among one another and insurgents have become less conspicuous.

The majority of the residents in Now Zad were Ishaqzai, who lived both in the DC and in the mountains to the north since the 19th Century. They were originally from Pusht Rod in Farah. During the reign of Abdul Rahman Khan in the 9th Century, the Ishaqzai were promised land in Badghis, but the migration failed and the Ishaqzai were forced to return. However in the meantime other people had settled on the original Ishaqzai land, causing severe land disputes when the Ishaqzai returned. The Ishaqzai were forced to resettle on less profitable land in Northern Helmand, such as Now Zad.

The US-led irrigation development projects in Helmand in the 1950s offered the Ishaqzai opportunities to return to Helmand, however they are by the original residents seen as the *Naqilin* or immigrants. These events have caused disenfranchisement and deep anti-GIRoA sentiments within the Ishaqzai tribe. Other tribes have reasons for having anti-GIRoA sentiments as well.

From 2001-2005 the Helmand Provincial Governor Sher Mohammad Akhundzada and his Provincial Chief of Police, Abdul Rahman Jan, installed DGs and DCOPs in Helmand loyal to themselves, and over this five year period they were responsible for severe abuse of the population, disenfranchising many people in Now Zad from GIRoA among all tribes.

The current District Governor, Sayed Murad Saadat, took his position in 2009 after the USMC cleared the District Centre. His deputy, Sayed Abdul Qayum, took up his post in February 2011. The DCOP Capt Attaullah Khan (removed from office and transferred to the provincial capital in mid-January 2012) is a respected farmer who joined the ANP after the Taliban withdrew. He is very knowledgeable on the District and its people.

There is no District Community Council (DCC) in Now Zad, nor is there a District Delivery Plan (DDP). It is the intention that IDLG is to perform an assessment in Now Zad, likely in April 2012, for the purpose of evaluating the possibility of establishing a DCC. Following that the task will be to develop a DDP. There is a judge and are two prosecutors in the District. There was, until quite recently, a *huquq* (civil disputes) as well. Despite the presence of these justice actors and the improved quality of the District Governor, it is quite likely that the population still frequently refers to Taliban for justice and dispute resolution.

Now Zad is an agricultural society, relying on a Karez fed water irrigation system. Before the Soviet occupation Now Zad was a net exporter of food. Today the farmers mainly grow poppy and wheat. The also grow watermelons, musk melons, apples, figs, almonds, apricots, grapes, corn, pomegranates, marijuana, walnuts, and miscellaneous vegetables. Many fruits and vegetables, however, are imported from Pakistan. Many items are imported from large markets such as Gereshk, Kandahar, and Lashkar Gah. Fuel tends to be imported from Iran/Herat.

The Now Zad area is not connected to the Helmand River. Instead a Karez system is employed -- hundreds of years old -- to supply water to the irrigation system. To stay functional, the Karez system requires regular maintenance in the form of clearing of silt, dirt and damages needs repairing. The water table has lowered possibly as a result of a decade of reduced precipitation (drought), the introduction of many more wells (hundreds in the last decade) and generator-operated water pumps, and reliance on flood irrigation techniques.

The security situation in the Now Zad District Center (DC) is permissive. The DC enjoys a higher degree of peace and security than almost any other population center in Helmand Province. There have been no SIGACTs in the DC in more than eight months. Outside the DC, IEDs are widespread and the primary threat. At least eight armed personnel in full Protective Posture Equipment (PPE), a corpsman, and a man-portable Electronic Counter-measure (ECM) are required in order to conduct dismounted patrols in the DC.

The Battle Space Owner (BSO) – a company commander in this case – has consolidated his forces at the Forward Operating Base (FOB) located in the DC. His focus is on maintaining the current security perimeter, promoting ANSF development, transitioning the lead for security to ANSF, and improving security along the main north/south route (the Landay Nawa Road) in the District. It is possible that BSO will opt to conduct disruption operations in the future.

ENDSTATE
"By mid-2013, Now Zad DC and its surrounding areas are secure, governed by GIRoA, and there is free and easy access to the wholesale market in Gereshk. The dispersed population has started to relocate to Now Zad and economic activity in the District is improving. The District Administration is executing its on-budget DDP, delivering some basic services in the form of education and health services to the population. The population has access to more advanced social services in Musa Qala, Gereshk or Lashkar Gah." – Now Zad *Annual Plan, 2011-2012*

APPENDIX - E
Random Thoughts from a Civil Affairs Team Leader
Capt. Michael C. Petit (USMC)

If there is anything that needs to be conveyed about this place (Now Zad District, Helmand Province) it is perhaps that things are not hopeless. Despite the violence and the drugs and the corruption and the poverty, the country is not hopeless and the people certainly are not. It is frustrating, infuriating at times, to consider how much time we have spent here – how much money and how many lives – and how little progress we have received in return for our costly investments. Certainly the Afghans are partially to blame for this dismal state of affairs. I would posit, however, that the international community bears most of the responsibility. For quite often the international community has elected to operate and invest in this country in a haphazard, misguided, and irresponsible manner.

Of the three primary civilians operating here in the Now Zad DST, two contributed minimally and one was absolutely invaluable. Those whose contributions were minor were great people, but they were gone so often and displayed such limited initiative that they achieved very little. This is a prime example of inefficiency and government funds poorly invested.

At a lunch a few months ago, a visiting battalion commander proclaimed to the District Governor: "You know, Governor, we Marines are here to fight and provide security. We just do some of this other stuff because we are nice." Messages like that coming from senior leaders help to explain the mess on the ground, widespread confusion, and limited progress and much as stories of Afghan apathy and corruption.

--- The international community lacks a common vision and clearly stated objectives. There is a great deal of inefficiency and waste, some of which is due, quite simply, to confusion over what we are trying to achieve.
--- It is not about how much time we spend here, how many lives are sacrificed, how many dollars are spent – it is about what we actually do while here on the ground. Throwing piles of money and lots of people at a problem does not guarantee that the problem will be solved. Ever.
--- Success depends on a positive, shared, effective philosophy and adequate resources, authority, and autonomy. And luck.
--- We – the military in particular – are becoming increasingly centralized and risk averse. This is not likely to lead to success along any line of operation.
--- The Afghans actually require very little material and manpower support. They do need a fair amount of financial assistance.
--- Our estimate is that the District government will require an annual budget of approximately 50,000 USD in order to survive and prevent the District from returning to Taliban control. After "investing" millions of dollars in this District, we now do not know if the international community is going to be able to provide this vital, meager funding. To provide perspective: the international

community has funded multiple projects in Now Zad that have been in the range of 300,000 - 750,000 USD.

--- Afghans must be given the space, the opportunity, to lead and manage their own affairs. We should insist that they bear responsibility, take credit for successes, and make their own decision and manage their own resources. We should supervise and provide counsel when necessary, allowing them to exercise control, mature, and grow comfortable in positions of power while the international community is still nearby and capable of lending a hand when required.

--- Our military, for the most part, either wants to completely run the show (development, governance, and security) – discounting the advice or completing excluding civilian experts and relegating Afghans leaders to figurehead roles. Or they want to have nothing to do with anything other than the security line of operations, and even then there is a tendency to pay only limited attention to the development of Afghan National Security Forces (ANSF). See bullet point #1.

--- Corruption. Everyone claims it is a major issue – perhaps the issue. It does exist to a degree. It helps to remember that patronage systems have been in place here for a long, long time, though, and this is not the only place in the world where organizations are tithed and individuals receive kickbacks.

--- Dependency and lack of initiative. If a parent offered her child an allowance of 1,000 USD a week, does anyone think that the child would ever say: "No, thank you. 20 USD will suffice"? Or, after a certain age, is it likely that the child would insist that the parent stop providing weekly payments? Our actions and the manner we have spent money – large sums of money – have greatly contributed to the problems of dependency and entitlement that we currently face. The international community is the parent that is shocked his child has yet to refuse an allowance payment.

--- The Afghans should not be blamed if the US government over pays for a contract. It is the person who negotiated the contract who should be held responsible.

--- The military – the Marines in particular -- are loath to take on stabilization/development/government mentoring roles. Although this is part of our cultural heritage and there is historical precedent, Marines generally lack both desire and expertise when it comes to these activities. Paying proper attention to these matters is essential, though, as there will be no transition or long term stability without a functional government and basic services for the local population to access. Perhaps the military should acknowledge this, willingly shoulder the burden, and take steps to be better prepared for the associated responsibilities.

APPENDIX - F
Recommendations for Civil Affair Teams
Capt Michael C. Petit (USMC)

Warning: Military personnel are likely to be the only readers who may find this section to be of any interest.

Respect the primacy of civilian leadership. If we wish to see a civilian-led, Afghan government with an organic system of checks and balances, ensure that one's actions do not empower ANSF leaders at the expense of GIRoA, civilian leadership. Similarly, CA Marines – and other military members -- may have to check instinctive tendencies to publicly demonstrate leadership and take charge of situations. They should, through their actions, set the example of a military force operating in support of political objectives and under civilian control. Military personnel, CA or otherwise, should avoid taking the lead on governance/political matters and instead defer to civilian partners in the DST.

Use CERP or other funds sparingly and precisely, being mindful of the possibility of distorting the local economy, causing rather than mitigating instability, contributing to corruption, and creating the expectation of and dependence on international support in general and financial support in particular.

Use these funds instead as a way of allowing the GIRoA officials to practice governing, provide basic services to the people of the District, and further develop their capacity to provide good governance. Time spent mentoring District leaders will likely prove more profitable in the long run than any collection of CERP/infrastructure development projects executed during a single deployment cycle.

Do not focus on projects for their own sake. Have a definite sense of how any money spent or project supported will aid us and/or our Afghan partners. What is the commander's/Stab Ad's endstate – and will this help to achieve it? We must ensure that we get something from every exchange. There has to be a "quid pro quo" mindset. A likely return on an investment must justify any corresponding resource expenditures. Think in terms of what the Afghans will be able to sustain upon our departure, what investments will be most likely to yield enduring, positive results.

Understand the environment before seeking to alter it through "development." Have a sense of what predecessors have done and of the effects of their actions and investments.

Attempt to take into consideration the likely long-term effects of your actions and investments. For example, in the past "cash for work" type projects/programs drew people to the District center. Laborers found short-term work but not sustainable employment and their presence also served to further strain an already limited and inadequate water supply.

Seek to develop more than just the physical infrastructure of the District. Strive to develop government capacity and capability. Endeavor to develop individuals, habits, outlooks, and processes that support transition and will contribute to enduring peace, stability, and prosperity in the region.

Ensure GIRoA is aware and supportive of all development projects in the District. To the people of the District, it should appear as though all good things -- all projects and development activities -- are the result of efforts made by GIRoA and District leaders on behalf of the people of the District.

Negotiate contract prices. Always. It is expected. A good starting point is to cut the price of the initial bid in half. Strive to pay a "fair" price. Do not waste or use taxpayer dollars in a frivolous or ineffective manner. Overpaying for contracts/goods/services will contribute to the existing problems of inflation, dependency, corruption, and entitlement.

Be ethical and equitable and mindful of existing balances of power. Ensure that projects are not always benefitting the same individuals, tribes, and/or communities. Without ignoring or discounting human factors, think quantitatively and capture and share data.

This is what will allow us to measure the relative effectiveness of our actions and investments.

Shun the spotlight. The goal is not to become popular or be fondly remembered by the Afghans. The goal is to affect positive change, promote stability, and facilitate the transition of responsibility to GIRoA and ANSF. This can be accomplished from the shadows and without fanfare.

Allow and encourage Afghan leaders to take credit for successes and responsibility for the affairs of the District in general. Grant government officials the opportunity to exercise responsibility, wield influence, and demonstrate their understanding of the fact that they are accountable to the people of the District and to the provincial government.

Empower Afghan leaders while providing supervision and support/mentoring as required. Frequently remind the people of the District that your role is neither to lead nor care for them. They have their own leaders. The role of the CA team is to support those leaders so that they, in turn, might respond to the needs of the people.

The Afghans will accept no for an answer. The import things are to be ethical and consistent. Integrity is of the utmost importance. Afghans are not likely to take matters personally provided that you do not first make the matter personal.

Get people to seek support from their leaders and encourage local leaders to lead – to enjoy the spotlight, take responsibility, demonstrate accountability, and receive credit for success. Do not provide support – in the form of CERP funding or otherwise – that can or should be provided by GIRoA. The goal is to get the Afghan system to mature to the point that it can function with at least a moderate degree of effectiveness.

Strengthen the links that exist between the District government and the people of the District. Encourage people or their elders to regularly meet with the District Governor and the other members of the District government. Encourage them to participate more fully in government by attending shuras, raising issues, and supporting projects.

Strengthen the ties that bind the District government to the provincial government. The relationship between these echelons of government is critical to the survival of the District government and to maintaining a District that is relatively free of insurgent activity and influence.

When LNs request support or ask for a project, some questions to ask of them are:
--- Can you and/or your community address this issue, e.g. karez repair, at your level? If not, why not?
--- Have you brought this matter to the attention of your village or tribal elder and/or the District government?
--- Why should CF assist you in this manner?
When LNs request support or ask for a project, some questions to ask of the CF unit are:
--- Is this project necessary? Is it vital or merely enhancing?
--- Is the contractor asking a reasonable price?
--- Is the contractor actually capable of doing the work? Does he possess the required expertise?
--- If we support the project/provide assistance, how will this benefit CF/ANSF, i.e. what is our return on investment? Goodwill? Fewer SIGACTs? ANSF recruits?
--- Is the project sustainable? By whom and how will it be sustained?
--- Is the project likely to yield positive, lasting results?

APPENDIX - G
NATO Bases as Wealth Spreading Machines
From: Metin Tarcan (2009)

Let's take a brigade level unit with 2,000 soldiers locked in a container-like base in Afghanistan. Assuming that the lines of logistic support are perfect, the soldiers of this brigade still want to spend money since shopping is a social phenomenon that comforts people in times of stress. If each soldier spends, on average, 200 USD a month on local food, souvenirs, and other needs during his or her deployment, it totals 400,000 USD in cash flow to the local markets monthly. Let's add subcontractors, who conduct small business for the brigade, and assume that they earn 100,000 USD monthly, and add the payments of the intelligence community of that brigade for the valuable tips from the informers and collaborators and assume that they earn 30,000 USD monthly. Let's add the gifts given to the local community leaders in the area of the responsibility of that brigade to make them happy and comfortable and assume that they are worth 20,000 USD monthly. Additionally, let's add the equipment and gear given to the locals to be used during operations or training, the end point of which is the local black market, and assume that they are worth 10,000 USD monthly. The total contribution of this brigade to the local economy is nearly 550,000 USD monthly.

REFERENCES

Abbaszadeh, N., Crow, M., El-Khoury, M., Gandomi, J., Kuwayama, D., MacPherson, C., Nutting, M., Parker, N., Weiss, T. 2008. Provincial Reconstruction Teams: Lessons and Recommendations. January 2008. Princeton University Report, 1-52.

Address by Barack Obama, President, United States of America. How we will complete our mission. Delivered at Bagram Air Base, Kabul, Afghanistan. May 2, 2012.

Afghan diaspora, 2010. Available at: www.afghandiaspora.ru

AIAS, 2008. Afghanistan's other neighbors: Iran, Central Asia, and China. Conference Report by the American Institute of Afghanistan Studies and the Hollings Center for International Dialogue, Istanbul, Turkey. July 2008.

Armstrong, R.L. & others, 2010. The glaciers of the Hindu Kush-Himalayan region: a summary of the science regarding glacier melt/retreat in the Himalayan, Hindu Kush, Karakoram, Pamir, and Tien Shan mountain ranges.

Baldauf, S. 2012. US legacy in Afghanistan: What 11 years of war has accomplished. Christian Science Monitor, June 10, 2012.

Benham, A.J., Kova´c˘, P., Petterson, M.G., Rojkovic, I., Styles, M.T.,Gunn, A.G., McKervey, J.A. and Wasy, A. 2009. Chromite and PGE in the Logar Ophiolite Complex, Afghanistan. Applied Earth Science (Trans. Inst. Min. Metall. B), 118 (2), 45-58.

Berman, E., Callen, M., Felter, J. H., and Shapiro, J. N. 2011. Do Working Men Rebel? Insurgency and Unemployment in Afghanistan, Iraq and the Philippines. Journal of Conflict Resolution, 55 (4), 496-528.

Blanchard, C.M. 2007. Afghanistan: narcotics and US policy. In: L.V. Barton, ed. Drugs and governmental policies. New York: Nova Science Publishers, 113p.

Bird, T and Marshall, A. 2011. Afghanistan: How the West lost its way. Yale University Press, New Haven.

Brahimi, A. 2010. The Taliban's evolving ideology. LSE Global Governance Working Paper, WP 02/2010. University of Oxford.

Burgess, R.R. 2006. Beneath the Surface: A Navy flight squadron conducts a geological survey of Afghanistan. Seapower, November 2006, 20-22.

Burki, S.K. 2011. The Creeping Wahhabization in Pashtunkhwa: The Road to 9/11. Comparative Strategy, 30, 154–176.

Chorev, M., and Sherman, J. 2010. The Prospects for Security and Political Reconciliation in Afghanistan: Local, National, and Regional Perspectives. Workshop Report, May 2010. Belfer Center for Science and International Affairs, Harvard Kennedy School.

CIA World Factbook. Available at: https://www.cia.gov/library/publications/the-world-factbook/

Coburn, N., and Dempsey, J. 2010. Informal Dispute Resolution in Afghanistan. United States Institute of Peace (USIP), Special Report, August 9, 2010.

Cordesman, A.H. 2010. How America corrupted Afghanistan; Time to look in the Mirror. Revised September 9, 2010. Center for Strategic and International Studies, Washington, DC.

Cullather, N. 2002. Damming Afghanistan: Modernization in a Buffer State. Journal of American History 89 (2), 512-537, September 2002.

Danovic, N. 2012. You Can't Play Chess When the Taliban is Playing Poker. Small Wars Journal. January 5, 2012.

Dawn News Report, 2011. Brig Ali Khan, four army officers convicted over Hizbut Tahrir links. Available at http://dawn.com/news/739474/brig-ali-khan-four-other-officers-convicted-in-mutiny-case

Dearing, M. 2008. Examining the Suicide Terror Movement in Afghanistan. The Culture & Conflict Review, 2 (3), Summer 2008.

Dressler, J. 2012. The Haqqani Network; A strategic threat. The Institute for the Study of War, Afghanistan Report 9.

Fair, C.C. 2010. India in Afghanistan and Beyond: Opportunities and Constraints. A Century Foundation Report, New York.

Feinstein, P., and Wilder, A. 2012. Winning Hearts and Minds? Examining the Relationship between Aid and Security in Afghanistan. January 2012. Feinstein International Center, Tufts University, Somerville, Massachusetts.

Gleason, G, Hanks, R.R., and Bosin, Y. 2009. Afghanistan reconstruction in regional perspective. Central Asian Survey, 28 (3), 275–287, September 2009.

Goepner, E.W. 2012. Battered Spouse Syndrome; How to Better Understand Afghan Behavior. U.S. Air Force Military Review, 59-66, January-February 2012.

Goodson, L., and Johnson, T.H. 2011. Parallels With The Past – How the Soviets lost in Afghanistan, How the Americans are losing. Foreign Policy Research Institute, *E-Notes,* April 2011.

Gordon, S. 2011. Winning Hearts and Minds? Examining the Relationship between Aid and Security in Afghanistan's Helmand Province. April 2011. Feinstein International Center, Tufts University, Somerville, Massachusetts.

Gray, J. 2011. War will not cease, if only because conflicts over natural resources are certain to increase (Perpetual warfare). Cover Story, New Statesman, September 5, 2011.

Griffiths, J.C. 2001. Afghanistan: A History of Conflict. Carlton Books, London, 66p.

Hadley, S., and Podesta, J. 2012. The Right Way Out of Afghanistan. Foreign Affairs, 91 (4). Jul/Aug 2012.

Hein, J., and Niazi, T. 2009. A Well-Founded Fear: The Social Ecology of 21st Century Refugees. Harvard International Review, Fall 2009, 38-42.

Historical Atlas of the British Empire, 2013. Available at: http://www.atlasofbritempire.com/Height_of_Empire.html

Hurst, C.A. 2010. China's Ace in the Hole; Rare Earth Elements. Joint Force Quarterly, 59, 4th quarter, 121-126.

Hussain, Z. 2013. The Scorpion's Tail: The relentless rise of Islamic militants in Pakistan and how it threatens America. Free Press. Institute for the Study of War, 2009. Available at: http://www.understandingwar.org/map/afghanistans-ethno-linguistic-groups

Ignatius, D. 2013. Afghanistan's improving ways. Washington Post, January 16, 2013. Available at: http://articles.washingtonpost.com/2013-01-16/opinions/36384610_1_afghanistan-saad-mohseni-kandahar

Isby, D. 2011. Afghanistan: Graveyard of empires, a new history of the borderland. Pegasus Books, New York.

Kaldor, M. 2007. New and Old Wars: Organized Violence in a Global Era. Stanford University Press; 2nd edition.

Kakar, P. 2004. Tribal Law of Pashtunwali and Women's Legislative Authority. Available at: http://www.law.harvard.edu/programs/ilsp/research/kakar.pdf

Kirk, T. 2011. Afghanistan: Reconciliation plans, tribal leaders and civil society. Small Wars Foundation. January 4, 2011.

Klare, M.T. 2007. Geopolitics Reborn: Oil, Natural Gas, and Other Vital Resources. New England Journal of Public Policy, 21 (2), 202-214.

Korf, B. 2011. Resources, violence and the telluric geographies of small wars. Progress in Human Geography, 35(6), 733–756.

Kronstadt, K.A. 2010a. Direct overt U.S. Aid and military reimbursements to Pakistan, FY2002-FY2011. Congressional Research Service report, 9 March 2010.

Kronstadt, K.A. 2010b. Major U.S. arms sales and grants to Pakistan since 2001. US Congressional Research Service report, March 23, 2010.

Liveleak, 2012. Available at: http://www.liveleak.com/view?i=0c1_1353986907#DtU4cvmTq98YOZsG.99

Lyon, D. 2008. Afghanistan: A New Great Game. New Statesman, January 3, 2008.

Maass, C.D. 2011. Afghanistan's Drug Career: Evolution from a War Economy to a Drug Economy. German Institute for International and Security Affairs, March 2011.

Mackenzie, J., 2011. Watershed of Waste: Afghanistan's Kajaki Dam and USAID. Available at: http://www.globalpost.com/dispatch/news/regions/asia-pacific/afghanistan/111007/watershed-waste-afghanistan%E2%80%99s-kajaki-dam-and-u

MacKenzie, J. 2011. The battle for Afghanistan militancy and conflict in Helmand. Counterterrorism Strategy Initiative Policy Paper. September 2010, New America Foundation.

Mahmood, T. 2010. Colonial cartographies and postcolonial borders: the unending war in and around Afghanistan. Available at: http://works.bepress.com/tayyab_mahmud/1

Malevich, J. J., and Youngman, D.C. 2011. The Afghan balance of power and the culture of Jihad. Military Review, May-June 2011, 33 – 39.

Maps of World, 2013. Available at: http://www.mapsofworld.com/

Mars, J.C., and Rowan L.C. 2011. ASTER spectral analysis and lithologic mapping of the Khanneshin carbonatite volcano, Afghanistan. Geosphere, 7 (1), 276–289.

Patterson, R., and Robinson, J. 2011. The Commander as Investor; Changing CERP Practices. Prism 2 (2) Features, 115-126. March 1, 2011.

Perry-Castañeda Library Map Collection at the University of Texas. Available at: www.lib.utexas.edu

Peters, G. 2009. How opium profits the Taliban. United States Institute of Peace (USIP), Peaceworks, 62.

Peterson, S. 2013. Why a dam in Afghanistan might set back peace. The Christian Science Monitor, July 30, 2013. Available at: http://www.csmonitor.com/World/Asia-South-Central/2013/0730/Why-a-dam-in-Afghanistan-might-set-back-peace

Randall, D., and Owen, J. 2012. An IoS investigation: To the Chinese and the Indians, the spoils of a terrible war. The Independent, March 18, 2012.

Rashid, A. 2000. Taliban. Yale University Press, New Haven, CT.

Roberts, A. 2009. Doctrine and Reality in Afghanistan. Survival, 51 (1), 29–60, February–March 2009.

Ross, M.L. 2004. How do natural resources influence civil war; evidence from thirteen cases. International Organization, 58, Winter 2004, 35-67.

Rubin, B.R., and Rashid, A. 2009. From Great Game to Grand Bargain: Ending Chaos in Afghanistan and Pakistan. Foreign Affairs, 87 (6), 30–44.

Sarkar, J., 2011. Monitoring Himalayan glaciers. *Current Science*, 101(5), pp.598–599.

Sarikaya, M.A. et al., 2012. Space-Based Observations of Eastern Hindu Kush Glaciers between 1992 and 2007, Afghanistan and Pakistan. Remote Sensing Letters, 3(1), 77–84.

Scheel, M., Frey, H., and Bolch, T. 2009. Report on the current distribution of glaciers in the Hindu Kush - Himalayan Region. University of Geneva, Switzerland. HighNoon Technical Report No 1.9.

Sharp, T. 2007. Resource conflict in the Twenty-First century. Peace Review: A Journal of Social Justice, 19, 323–330.

Shroder, J.F. 1976. Regional distribution of physical resources in Afghanistan. Unpublished report delivered at University of Nebraska, Omaha – USAID Conference on Afghanistan.

Shroder, J.F. 1981. Physical resources and the development of Afghanistan. Studies in Comparative International Development, 36-63, Fall-Winter, 1981.

Simpson, S. 2011. Afghanistan's Buried Riches. Scientific American, 305 (4), 58-64.

Sims, C. 2012. Fighting the Insurgents' War in Afghanistan. Small Wars Journal, Jan 12 2012.

Stavridis, J.G. 2011. The comprehensive approach in Afghanistan. Prism 2 (2), 65-76.

Stenersen, A. 2010. The Taliban insurgency in Afghanistan – organization, leadership and worldview. Norwegian Defense Research Establishment (FFI) 5 February 2010.

Strickland, R.C. 2007. The way of the Pashtun: Pashtunwali. The Canadian Army Journal, 10.3, 44-55, Fall 2007.

Sukumaran, P.V. 2012. The need to explore for rare earth minerals. Current Science, 102 (6).

Tanner, S. 2002. Afghanistan: A Military History from Alexander the Great to the Fall of the Taliban. Da Capo Press, Cambridge, MA.

Tierney, J. F. 2010. Warlord, Inc. Extortion and Corruption along the U.S. Supply Chain in Afghanistan. Report of the Majority Staff Rep. John F. Tierney, Chair Subcommittee on National Security and Foreign Affairs Committee on Oversight and Government Reform U.S. House of Representatives, June 2010.

Turcan, M. 2009. Between heaven and earth: Field observations relating to counterinsurgency in tribalized rural Muslim environments. Dynamics of Asymmetric Conflict, 2 (2), 86–111.

Vogt, H. 2013. Kajaki Dam Project: US pushes to finish Afghan dam as challenges mount. Available at: http://www.huffingtonpost.com/2013/01/05/kajaki-dam_n_2415738.html

Waldman, M. 2010. The Sun in the Sky: The relationship between Pakistan's ISI and Afghan insurgents. Carr Center for Human Rights Policy, Kennedy School of Government, Harvard University.

Wan, K.W. 2011. Tethys leads charge into Afghanistan. Petroleum Economist, 78 (7).

Wegerich, K. 2010. The Afghan water law: "A legal solution foreign to reality"? Water International, 35 (3), 298–312.

West, B. 2011. The Wrong War: Grit, Strategy and the way out of Afghanistan. Random House, New York.

Wilber, D.N. 1953. Afghanistan, Independent and Encircled. Foreign affairs, 486-494, April 1953.

Wright, E. 2009. Generation Kill. Corgi Books, London, 35p.

INDEX

A

Abdul Rashid Dostum, 28
Afghan conflict, 1, 8, 24, 45
Afghan corruption, 128, 176
Afghan Geological Survey, vii
Afghan Local Police, vii, 118
Afghan National Army, vii, 117, 119
Afghan National Civil Order Police, vii
Afghan National Police, vii, 117
Afghan National Security Forces, iv, vii, 90, 199
Afghan refugees, 22, 43
Afghan Reintegration and Reconciliation Program, vii, 131
Afghan security forces, 118, 121
Afghan Society, ii, xix
Afghan soil, 5, 17, 23, 24, 49, 50, 91, 94, 111, 181
Afghan Transit Trade, vii, 14
Afghan tribes, 4, 13, 49
Afghan Uniformed Police, vii, 117
Afghan war, v, vi, 4, 5, 22, 23, 24, 26, 94, 103, 108, 148, 162, 171, 175, 176
Afghan War Asymmetry, iv, 90
Afghans, vi, xvii, 5, 14, 19, 22, 24, 27, 28, 36, 43, 44, 49, 67, 79, 80, 87, 94, 100, 102, 104, 105, 106, 111, 122, 124, 125, 129, 131, 147, 148, 149, 150, 152, 153, 154, 159, 160, 166, 168, 169, 178, 180, 181, 185, 197, 198, 199, 200, 201, 202, 203
Afghan-Soviet Treaty of Friendship, 17
AGS, vii, 68
Ahmad Shah Abdali, 9
Aiman Alzawahiri, 31, 38

Al-Azhar University, 24
Alexander 'The Great', 49
ALP, vii, 118, 119, 148, 169
Al-Qaeda, 31, 43, 91, 99, 103, 128, 165, 180
Amanullah Khan, 5, 17
ambulance, xvi, 155, 157, 158
Amir Abdul Rehman, 12
Amirul Momineen, 29, 190
Amu Darya, x, 17, 43, 63, 64
ANA, vii, 117, 118, 123, 132, 140
ANCOP, vii, 117
Anglo-Afghan, 4, 5
ANP, vii, xiv, 117, 118, 122, 195
ANSF, vii, 113, 117, 118, 119, 121, 122, 123, 131, 162, 174, 181, 196, 199, 200, 202, 204
appeasement, 13
aquifer, xiii, 80
Area of Operation, vii
ARRP, vii, 131, 132, 174
Asian Development Bank, 44
Asymmetric Development, iv, 90
ATT, vii, 14
AUP, vii, xiii, xvii, 95, 117, 118, 132, 140, 148, 179
Ayatullah Khomeni, 21
Aynak copper deposit, 61

B

Babrak Karmal, 19, 21, 26
Bachae Saqaw, 18
Badakhshan, 2, 62, 65
Bagram Air Base, 148, 187, 206
Baluchistan, 42, 77
Bamiyan *Buddhas*, 97
Bangladesh, vii, 3, 7, 155, 191

Bangladesh Rural Advancement Committee, vii, 155
battle of Plassey, 3
Battle Space Owner, vii, 196
bazar, xiii, 75
beauty parlor, xvi, 140, 145, 146
bipolar world, 26
boundary commission, 7
British, x, 4, 5, 6, 7, 8, 9, 12, 13, 14, 17, 34, 49, 66, 72, 78, 115, 147, 148, 171, 189, 190, 209
British colonial era, 3
British Crown, 3
British India Act, 4
BSO, vii, 148, 159, 173, 196
buffer zone, 9, 12, 13
Burhanuddin Rabbani, 23, 28
Buzkashi, 97

C

CAG, vii, 77, 78, 148, 155, 171
Camp Leatherneck, xii, 69, 70, 80, 148, 155, 187
Cannabis, xiv, 110
Capt, vii, xviii, 77, 113, 118, 121, 128, 147, 150, 153, 155, 165, 166, 169,
Carbonatite, 59
CARs, iii, vii, xix, 1, 40, 44, 61
Caspian Sea, 44, 87
census, 1, 33
Central Asia, 121, 189, 206
Central Asian, vii, 1, 25, 31, 44, 92, 94, 108, 115, 208
Central Asian Republics, vii, 1, 44, 108
Central Intelligence Agency, vii
CERP, vii, 78, 147, 149, 201, 203, 212
CF, vii, 42, 119, 121, 140, 153, 154, 160, 170, 173, 204
Chechen fighters, 72

China, iii, xix, 1, 2, 8, 40, 45, 46, 59, 61, 63, 66, 73, 87, 106, 183, 206, 209
church and state, 190
CIA, vii, 1, 24, 25, 31, 135, 207
Civil Affairs, vi, vii, xviii, 173, 197
climate change, 76, 78
Coalition Forces, vii, 140, 148, 160, 176
COIN, vii, 24, 99, 100
Cold War, ii, xix, 1, 17, 18, 24, 26
Commander's Emergency Response Program, vii
copper, x, 50, 57, 61, 62, 66
Counter Insurgency, vii, 99
Coups, ii, xix
culture of entitlements, 150

D

DACAAR, vii, 76
dam, xii, xiii, 43, 44, 71, 72, 73, 76, 82, 83, 84, 211, 212, 214
Dari, 15, 34, 135
Day of Judgment, 188
DCOP, vii, 77, 119, 122, 129, 131, 194, 195
Deobandi, 38
DG, vii, xiv, xvi, 112, 114, 122, 129, 140, 146, 149, 151, 155, 157, 173
DoD, viii, 123, 176, 187
dowry, 138
drone strikes, 43, 103
drug export, 14
DST, viii, xiii, 82, 148, 152, 197, 200
dug-wells, 76
Durand Line, ii, vi, x, xix, 2, 10, 12, 94
Durand line, 9
Durra, xiv, 97, 98

E

East India Company, viii, 3

Edward Snowden, 163
Egyptian Pharaohs, 50
empires, 3, 5, 210
Energy Resources, iii, 48
Energy resources, 63
Ethno-linguistic Groups, ii, xix
European, 3, 134
evapo-transpiration, 111

F

Farghana, 189
FATA, viii, 9, 12, 14, 94, 175, 191
fatwa, 112, 190
Female Engagement Team, viii, 140
forced migrations, 87
foreign policy, 4, 189
freedom fighters, 21
Freedom War, 4

G

Gemstones, iii, 48, 64
General Zia ul Haq, 22
Geneva Accord, 26
Geologic, x, 51, 52
geology, 50, 51
Geophysical, 59
geo-politics, 49
Geo-Politics, iii, 48
GIRoA, iv, viii, 90, 105, 108, 112, 113, 119, 128, 129, 130, 131, 132, 147, 148, 149, 152, 153, 155, 162, 169, 171, 173, 174, 194, 195, 197, 200, 201, 202, 203
Gold, 1, 62
Graveyard of Empires, v, 3, 39
Great Britain, 5
Great Game, 4, 5, 211, 212
Green on Blue, xvii, 178, 179
Ground Water, iii, 48, 76

H

Habibullah Kalakani, 18
Hafeezullah Amin, 21
Haji-Gak iron ore, 62
Haqqani network, 121, 163, 164, 208
HAVA, viii, 69, 72
Hazara, 22, 33
healthcare, xv, 16, 101, 139, 142, 181
Heavy Metal Deposits, iii, 48
Heavy metals, 61
Helmand, vi, viii, xii, xiii, xiv, xv, xvi, xviii, 25, 43, 45, 59, 67, 68, 69, 70, 72, 73, 78, 79, 82, 84, 99, 100, 102, 104, 107, 108, 109, 110, 111, 113, 115, 119, 122, 125, 126, 127, 128, 131, 140, 141, 145, 147, 148, 149, 152, 157, 169, 171, 187, 193, 194, 195, 196, 197, 209, 211
Helmand River, 71
Hillary Clinton, 92
Himalayas, 1, 50, 51
Hindu Kush, 1, 50, 65, 68, 206, 213
Hindu majority, 7
Hizbut Tehrir, 92
Hujra, 191
hygiene, xv, 141, 144

I

IED, viii, 101, 102
India, iii, viii, xix, 3, 4, 5, 7, 8, 9, 12, 13, 14, 40, 41, 44, 45, 49, 59, 65, 66, 76, 104, 106, 107, 121, 180, 181, 183, 189, 190, 191, 208
Indian Army, 4
Indian Mutiny, 4
Indian National Congress, 41
Indian Ocean, 14, 19, 21, 49
Indian subcontinent, 3, 4, 5, 189
Indus River, 9

Indus Valley, 9
insurgency, v, 34, 38, 42, 88, 90, 96, 97, 100, 102, 108, 119, 121, 152, 162, 163, 166, 180, 183, 193, 206, 213
Inter-tribal rivalries, 15
Iran, iii, xix, 1, 2, 21, 24, 40, 43, 46, 66, 69, 76, 87, 104, 106, 107, 108, 115, 135, 170, 176, 180, 183, 196, 206
ISAF, viii, xii, xiii, xiv, 11, 12, 13, 67, 69, 72, 73, 74, 82, 97, 99, 112, 120, 122, 124, 148, 149, 159, 166, 169, 170, 187
ISI, viii, 8, 23, 24, 25, 26, 30, 31, 42, 76, 91, 92, 94, 95, 103, 105, 162, 163, 164, 166, 214
Islam, 9, 31, 32, 34, 37, 38, 96, 97, 99, 111, 112, 134, 139, 154, 188, 190, 191
Islamabad, 8, 22, 92
Islamic Caliphate, 31
Islamic Emirates of Afghanistan, 30, 99
Islamic laws, 8
Islamic State, 17, 190
Islamist fundamentalism, 180
Islamization, 23

J

Jammu and Kashmir, 106
Jihad, 24, 100, 132, 211
Jihadi, 8, 9, 91, 99
Jihadi terrorists, 183
John Foster Dulles, 18

K

Kabul government, 182
Kajaki, iii, xii, 48, 71, 72, 73, 74, 169, 211, 214
Kandahar, xiii, xiv, 17, 29, 30, 59, 63, 70, 71, 72, 79, 85, 93, 94, 99, 107, 109, 111, 133, 135, 151, 154, 170, 178, 196
Karachi port, 14
Karakoram, 1, 206
Karez, 77, 78, 82,194, 195, 196, 204
Kashmir, viii, 7, 31, 86, 106, 107, 181
Khalq party, 19
Khan Nashin, xv, 59, 60, 66, 134
Khilafah, 9, 92, 104
Khushal Khan Khattak, 36
Khyber Pass, 3, 9, 32, 49, 189
Khyber Pukhtunkhwa, viii, 40, 164
King Zahir Shah, 18, 19, 24
Kochis, 133
kumak, 153

L

landlocked country, 1, 14, 117
lapis lazuli, 50, 64
Lashkar Gah, 71, 113, 133, 149, 151, 155, 193, 196, 197
Lenin, 17
Line of Control, viii, 7, 106
lithium, 49, 57
LoC, viii, 7
Loya Jirga, 2, 13, 93

M

M. A. Jinnah, 41
MAAWS-A, viii, 150
Maharaja, 7
Mahram, 138
margin of error, 33
Marines, xii, xvi, xvii, 25, 122, 128, 141, 144, 146, 148, 154, 158, 160, 167, 172, 173, 179, 188, 198, 200
Martial Law, 23, 190
Mashhad, 76
mass migration, 22

Maulana Sufi Muhammad, 190
Mazar-i-Sharif, 28, 133, 134, 135
Michael C. Petit, vi, xviii, 197, 200
micro-grants, 152
mineral development, x, 54, 65
Mineral exploitation, 87
Mineral Resources, iii, 48, 57
mineral wealth, vi, 49, 88, 106
Ministry of Agriculture, Irrigation and Livestock, 79
Ministry of Mines, viii, 61, 68
Modern Afghanistan, ii, xix
Mohammadzai tribe, 20
Money As A Weapon System, viii, 149, 150
Mongols, 9
mountains, 1, 65, 176, 194
Mountstuart Elphinstone, 36
Mughal Empire, 189
Mughal rule, 3
Mughals, 36, 49
Muhammad Bin Qasim, 189
Mujahideen, ii, xix, 21, 23, 24, 26, 28, 31, 93, 170, 171, 190
Mullah Omar, 29, 97, 99, 107, 112, 132, 162, 170
Mumbai Hotel attacks, 8
Musa Qala, 77, 131
Muslim League, 41
Muslim majority, 7
Muslim Ummah, 37

N

Najibullah, 26, 28, 29
NATO, iv, v, viii, xvi, 34, 45, 90, 92, 93, 94, 100, 101, 102, 123, 125, 139, 146, 160, 162, 163, 164, 165, 170, 205
natural gas, 44, 51, 63, 87

natural resources, v, vi, 5, 40, 68, 86, 87, 88, 209, 212
Nawab Akbar Bugti, 42
Neo-Conservative, 93
New Democracy Program, 19
Nimroz, 70, 107, 132, 184
non-governmental organizations, 159
Noor Muhammad Taraki, 19, 21
North Waziristan, 95
Now Zad, xiv, xvi, xviii, 46, 78, 105, 111, 113, 122, 128, 140, 146, 149, 150, 151, 155, 156, 169, 171, 173, 193, 194, 195, 196, 197, 199
nuclear neighbors, 8, 181
NWFP, viii, 40

O

Olaswal, 130
opium, 3, 30, 115, 212
Orogenic, 50
Osama Bin Laden, viii, 25, 91, 189
Oxus River, 9

P

Pakistan, ii, iii, vi, viii, ix, x, xix, 1, 3, 5, 7, 8, 9, 10, 12, 13, 14, 15, 21, 22, 23, 24, 26, 28, 30, 31, 37, 40, 41, 42, 44, 45, 46, 63, 76, 77, 87, 91, 92, 93, 94, 99, 103, 104, 105, 106, 107, 108, 115, 121, 163, 164, 166, 170, 180, 181, 183, 188, 191, 193,196, 209, 210, 212, 213, 214
Pakistan Army, 41
Palestinian conflict, 7
Pan-Islamist, 9
Panjsher Valley, 65
Parcham, 19
Pashto, 15, 29, 34, 36, 38, 135

Pashtun, v, 4, 9, 12, 13, 15, 34, 36, 37, 38, 96, 163, 190, 191, 213
Pashtunwali, ii, xix, 35, 36, 37, 38, 39, 210, 213
PDPA, 19, 20, 21
Pervez Musharraf, 27, 91
Peshawar, v, 22, 23, 24, 190
political reconciliation, 182
political solution, 182
poppy, xiv, 14, 30, 107, 108, 109, 110, 111, 113, 114, 131, 195
population explosion, 42
Prince Daud, 18, 19, 20
Provincial Reconstruction Teams, 159, 206
proxy war, 24, 181
PRTs, iv, 90, 159
Public hangings, 30
purely accidental state, 9

Q

Qatar, 37, 40, 132
QIPs, 159

R

Rare Earth Minerals, iii, 48, 50, 57
rebuilding, 8, 88
Red Army, xii, 21, 24, 25, 26, 31, 38
REEs, ix, 57, 58, 59
refugee camps, 22, 24, 30, 94
Regional Command, 121, 147
regional dialogue, 183
regional geography, 1
Regional Players, iii, xix
Regional Solution, iv, 90, 180
Reintegration, iv, vii, 90, 131
Religion, xviii, 188

religious, vi, 20, 21, 22, 23, 40, 41, 93, 94, 96, 99, 111, 134, 138, 154, 180, 191, 192
religious fundamentalism, 184
religious fundamentalists, 136
religious groups, 8
Republic of Afghanistan, 19, 21, 93
residual force, 162
resource curse, 88
Resource Wars, iii, 48
River, x, xi, xii, xiii, 4, 13, 43, 45, 64, 71, 73, 76, 84, 196
Russia, iii, xix, 1, 5, 17, 21, 30, 40, 45, 66, 87, 104, 106, 115
Russian, xii, 4, 18, 21, 24, 25, 26, 33, 164
Russian invasion, 21, 49

S

Saddam Hussein, 93, 175, 176
Salala incident, 92
Salma Dam, iii, 48, 71, 76
salt peter, 3
Saudi Arabia, 25, 30, 31, 37, 40, 49, 57, 181
security bubbles, 24
Security concerns, 66
seismic, 50
Shah Reza Pehlavi, 21
Sharia laws, 36
Shia religion, 33, 43, 46
Shura, xii, 10, 99, 148
Sibghatullah Mojaddadi, 23, 28
Sir Mortimer Durand, 1, 5, 12
Sistan wetland, 68
Society of Entitlement, 130
solar panels, 73
Soviet invasion, 1, 65, 134
Soviet Occupation, ii, xix
SRAD, ix, 79, 148

strategic depth, 24
Suicide bombings, 41
Sunni-Shia, 25
Swat, 9, 190

T

Taliban, ii, iv, v, ix, xii, xiii, xiv, xix, 15, 22, 29, 30, 31, 34, 37, 38, 40, 41, 42, 43, 60, 72, 74, 76, 78, 79, 87, 90, 92, 93, 94, 95, 96, 97, 98, 99, 100, 101, 102, 104, 107, 108, 111, 113, 118, 119, 121, 122, 123, 128, 131, 132, 134, 138, 139, 147, 160, 162, 163, 165, 166, 169, 170, 171, 173, 174, 176, 178, 180, 181, 184, 190, 191, 193, 194, 195, 198, 207, 208, 212, 213, 214
Talibanization, 22
target killings, 41
Tashkil, 153
tax payers money, 125
terrorism, 8, 16, 42, 91, 108, 163, 165
terrorist organization, 91, 121
Texas, xi, 1, 42, 212
The Way Forward, iv, 90
Thorium, 57, 58, 59
Timothy A. Noller, vi, 78, 123
Trans-Afghanistan pipeline, 44
tribal societies, 15, 18, 129, 154, 184
tribal structure, 15, 131
TTP, ix, 95, 99
TVA, 69
Two-Nation theory, 190

U

Ulema, 190
UN General Assembly, 13

United Nations, ix, 22, 33
Urdu, 15, 192
US Army, 148
USAID, ix, xii, xv, xvii, 69, 72, 73, 79, 127, 151, 152, 153, 176, 177, 211, 213
USDA, ix, 69, 111, 113, 153
USGS, ix, 51, 59, 63, 68
USMC, vi, viii, ix, xviii, 27, 66, 80, 111, 121, 123, 128, 148, 155, 169, 173, 193, 195, 197, 200
US-Mexico border, 13
USSR, ix, 17, 18, 19, 20, 24, 26, 45, 51, 91
Utra Tangi Island, 17

W

Wahabi, 37, 38, 134, 191
warlords, 28, 29, 61, 87, 123, 128
warm waters, 19, 21, 26, 49
Washington, i, vi, 42, 103, 106, 175, 207, 210
Water, iii, xii, 48, 68, 69, 70, 80, 214
water law, 70, 214
Water Resources, iii, 68
Weapons of Mass Destruction, 93, 175
West Pakistan, 7
Women Development, iv, 90
World Bank, 14
World War I, 5
World War II, 7
wrong war, 184

Z

Zahiruddin Muhammad Babar, 3, 189
Zulfiqar Ali Bhutto, 22